THE PARENTS' GUIDE TO
SWIMMING

by

Alan W. Arata, Ph.D.

ISBN: 1-4107-2538-3 (e-book)
ISBN: 1-4107-2539-1 (Paperback)

Library of Congress Control Number: 2003091531

This book is printed on acid free paper.

Printed in the United States of America
Bloomington, IN

Cover photograph by © David Black, 2003

1stBooks – rev. 06/11/03

CONTENTS

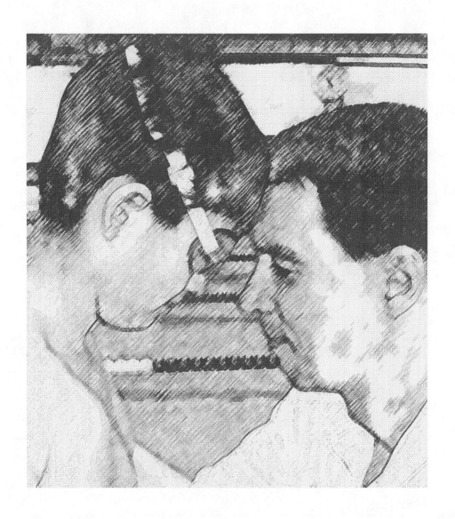

ONE

THE LIFE-LONG BENEFITS OF SWIMMING

Swimming is *the* most complete sport invented by man. As a Biomechanist, a former NCAA swimmer and coach, as well as the father of two age-group swimmers, I believe this to be true. A good swimmer performing any of the four strokes makes it look so simple, and yet learning to swim well is a balancing act of coordination and power that combines complex movement patterns fueled by aerobic and anaerobic energy systems of the body. As an art, swimming is four very different strokes and racing tactics. As a science, it is the physics of propulsion, drag, starts and turns, the psychology of be-lieving in one's abilities and the capacity to endure fatigue. All of the above make swimming one of the best activities, not to mention sports for children, no matter what their future goals may be. So, con-gratulations, you have chosen a great *sport*. What's more, you are concerned enough to pick up this *book* to learn about this great sport and what you can do to help your child succeed in it.

Now swimming is an individual sport, and though swimmers are on a team, it is still about one swimmer in the water facing his or her toughest competition. Without ever having seen any of your children swim in practice or in a meet, I know who their toughest competition is. It is they, themselves—their motivations and expectations are their greatest assets, but can also be their greatest liabilities. Swimmers are constantly struggling between the right thing to do, which can hurt but has long-term rewards, and the easy thing to do, which may have little negative *short*-term effect but few *long*-term *rewards* either. Swimming is fun and going fast is fun, but swimming workouts can be painful, both physically and psychologically. What's more, swimmers, if they work hard, bring this pain on themselves. The faster they go, the more it hurts. Yet they do all this today so that they can swim faster tomorrow. Many of life's really important challenges require this kind of delayed gratification. They require preparation, self-discipline and dedication to hard work. Children growing up today so often take *instant* gratification for granted. And we parents help perpetuate this with DVD players, VCRs, satellite or cable TV, computers and video games. When children want entertainment, they have it at their fingertips. Success in life, though, does not come with a remote control. Success takes long-term planning and hard work. Well, swimming requires this kind of self-discipline too. And once swimmers, as few other athletes can, learn the discipline of dedicating themselves to work, they can then take that skill outside the pool and apply it in the rest of their lives.

In addition to self-discipline, daily swimming workouts and competitive meets teach young swimmers persistence. For children to even *learn* to swim well, they face what must seem to be insurmountable odds. No one gets in the water and is a great swimmer right away. If a child had to be good at swimming to *start* swimming, no one would ever swim. As I said already, swimming is a mixture of complex movement patterns. In order to learn to swim, a person must undergo years of persistent training. The body movements for freestyle alone require bilateral arm movement (using both arms) synchronized to opposing bilateral leg movement. Additionally, each breath must be coordinated in this sequence so that the swimmer inhales air, not water. And beyond these obvious things lie intricate and technical movements like hand pattern and pitch to produce the most propulsion and reduce drag. If this process isn't difficult enough, children attempt to perfect swimming with ever-changing bodies, as some grow over 15% taller in the course of a single year. It is very easy for a beginner to get frustrated—but if they don't *quit*, they learn persistence. Once learned, this life skill will bring them success in other parts of their lives too, from school to work to marriage.

Persistence requires a goal. Goal setting is another life skill fostered by swimming. Swimmers learn to set goals, both short and long-term. Swimming is so goal-focused because everything is measured and timed. There are goals for every swimming set in every swimming workout and goals for every swimming race in every swimming meet. Pools have timing clocks to quantify swimmers' progress. Swimmers set short-term goals that require them to work hard and smart in practice to help achieve long-term goals of swimming well during meets or making qualifying times or competing to win championships. As swimmers grow older, they approach school the same way, setting goals for individual assignments in a class to achieve the larger goal of learning or a good grade. And beyond school, life and business follow suit and all because you, the smart parent, placed them on a swim team.

Sportsmanship, learning how to cope—win or lose, is another valuable skill that swimming can develop. Life has its ups and downs and kids need to learn how to deal with both successes and failures. In a swimming race with 40 swimmers, there is only one overall winner. If there are six heats in the race, then there are also six heat winners. Sooner or later, your child may win a heat, or even an event. Handling such success and being courteous about it is an important life behavior. It is good for children to learn to be gracious winners and good sports. With persistence towards set goals, swimming should provide them with this opportunity.

Now, whereas we all want our children to know how to *win* successfully and courteously, not all swimmers will *be* race winners or even heat winners. It is *just* as important, if not more so, to learn to be a good sport when you *don't* win. Life really isn't about being the winner. In school, there is only one person in the class with the highest grades; only one valedictorian in each graduating class. In a company there is only one CEO. The rest of us must learn how to fit in the middle somewhere. So do most swimmers. Even top swimmers in one event need to learn how to fit into the middle in other events. Sportsmanship is not only gracious winning, it is also gracious losing.

Then there is the ability to perform under stress. Think about what happens when swimmers stand on the starting blocks. For those of you who have had the dream where you find yourself in front of a class or a group in your underwear, this is pretty close to swimming. Swimmers stand on the starting block, clad in only a thin piece of Lycra, set to put themselves and their hard workouts on display for the public. Is there stress involved in this? You bet! A swimming career is filled with stress. Some of this stress is self-imposed while some comes from external sources like parents (yes, you), coaches and teammates. Swimmers must learn how to handle both of these types of stress in order to perform their best. Life itself is filled with stress from these same sources. When swimmers learn how to deal with standing on a starting block set to perform for the crowd with only a thin piece of Lycra covering them, they have learned more stress management than many adults.

The above mentioned skills have all been life lessons and "between the ears" changes that the sport of swimming can help to mold. Equally important is what swimming does for a child *physically*.

One of the most important physical changes that swimming bestows is in a child's coordination. As stated earlier, the stroke of freestyle requires bilateral coordination of the arms and legs. In order to master this primary stroke, children must develop movement patterns that engage the dominant and non-dominant sides of their bodies equally. Swimming may be the only sport that does this so well for both the arms and the legs. Because of this, the skill of swimming tends to cross over well into other physical activities. Swimmers often make better all around athletes than do athletes from other sports.

Another physical adaptation that occurs with swim training is muscle growth. This is a very positive thing for most swimmers. Skinny kids can become powerful men and women and heavy kids can be chiseled into lean and strong young adults. This can help your

4

swimmer's self-esteem, as appearance is very important to teenagers and adults alike.

Swimming also promotes aerobic fitness. Aerobic exercise has been linked with longer life, better health, lower stress and other life-long benefits. For years, the American College of Sports Medicine recommended 20 minutes of aerobic exercise three times a week to maintain good aerobic health. Recently, they have changed their stance on this and now recommend aerobic exercise for as much as *one hour a day, five days a week.* By the time swimmers are 12 years old, they are often swimming ninety minutes or more, five to six days a week. Swimming is one of very few sports an individual can perform during a lifetime that meets the American College of Sports Medicine's aerobic guidelines. Learning good fitness habits at a young age gives swimmers a great start for a lifestyle of healthy living, and swimming is a life-long sport even if competition is not the goal.

In addition to the mental and physical aspects already mentioned, there are side benefits to swimming that few people realize. One is simple cleanliness—children can't help but stay clean when they spend more than an hour a day in a swimming pool. Sooner or later, this cleanliness grows on them and even after leaving the sport of swimming, they still feel the need to stay clean. Unlike with other sports, parents don't usually have to fight to get their kids in the shower—after swimming practice, swimmers flock to the shower; it is one of the nice rewards. The only problem then is getting the kids *out* to go home.

Swimming can also be a lifesaver. Family vacations are often oriented around some type of water, whether it's the ocean, a lake, or even a water park. A swimmer who is competent in the water is much less of a risk or worry for the parents. This means everyone has more fun. In addition, a competent swimmer can rescue someone in distress in the water. Obviously, if the rescued loved one were yours, you would believe in swimming as a most important ability.

The last benefit to swimming covered in this book involves intelligence. Now I can't say this is a contributory relationship, but if you check collegiate GPAs of swim team members, you will discover that they are significantly higher than those of the student body in general and than those of other collegiate sport athletes. This may be because all the above-mentioned modifications accrued through swimming, once internalized, get applied to academics. (Then again, it may be that swimmers have genetically more intelligent parents—parents who are smart enough to put their children into the sport of swimming!) Whatever, the results are there. Swimmers are smarter.

So again, congratulations for producing a swimmer. Your child may never realize how much swimming will help in his/her life, whether they swim for 60 years or two, but now you will. I believe swimming, with its fostering and development of both life and physical skills is the best sport to develop a young child into a respectful, self-confidant and responsible adult. At last glance, we could use more such people in our world.

T W O

MENTAL STRENGTH

There are physical aspects to swimming and there are mental aspects. When children first start to swim, the physical aspects account for about 90% of their successes. As children perfect their swimming skills, however, the mental aspects become more and more predominant and the percentages switch. Even so, at the higher levels as well as with younger kids mental strength training for swimming (and other sports) is commonly overlooked. It is seldom intentionally taught to athletes by coaches or parents. One problem is the fact that it is not physical, like swimming a workout or lifting weights and therefore progress is not easily charted. Partly because of this, coaches most often work with the physical aspects of swimming such as technique and endurance. Coaches who do understand the importance of mental strength and want to implement mental strength training can really only be effective for 10 to 15 individuals because of time constraints alone. After all, actual swimming must be accomplished during workouts as well. I would guess there is more than a 15:1 swimmer to coach ratio on your child's team. Swim teams can't survive financially with lower numbers. Additionally, coaches may not understand the importance of mental strength, or even if they do, may not know how to foster it in their athletes while at the same time offering workouts. Understanding how to build and foster mental strength in

7

athletes is a rare ability that few individuals possess, including the highest paid professional coaches. This may not sound very promising, but I have purposely put this chapter on mental strength ahead of the physical training chapters because it *is* much more important in the long run.

The good news is that mental training is an area a parent can address. Who should know more about how your child's mind works than you. You are the right one for this job and the following sections are meant to help direct your words and actions to best encourage mental strength in your child.

The Body is Weak but the Mind is Strong

Two men run to the aide of another who is trapped under a helicopter. The helicopter has crashed into a stream and is slowly sinking. The pilot (a former competitive swimmer) is in shock and about to drown. A warning signal is beeping, indicating that fuel is leaking and the helicopter could explode at any moment. The two men run to help the pilot, ignoring the fuel leak indicator. Without thinking, one of them says, "I'll lift and you pull him out." The man bends down and gets a grip on one of the helicopter's door jams, and straining mightily, he lifts the aircraft up enough so that his companion can slide the trapped pilot to safety. While this is occurring, a woman with a video camera captures the miraculous rescue on film.

After the rescue, the news media gets a look at the video and interviews the man who lifted the helicopter. They say to him, "That helicopter weighed thousands of pounds (about 1,500 kg). How in the world were you able to lift it?" The man didn't really know, but answered, "It just had to be done."

Many people have heard stories like this one, about mothers lifting cars to get to their trapped children after auto accidents, etc. Feats such as these have several things in common. The most import is that the person performing the lift did something that no one thought was humanly possible. An Olympic weight lifter couldn't have lifted the helicopter if a gold medal had depended on it. A sports scientist could have assessed this man's strength potential and told us that there was no way he could have lifted a helicopter. But it happened. The human body is incredible and capable of amazing feats. *The body is strong.*

It's the mind that is weak. The story above illustrates a second thing. "That helicopter weighed thousands of pounds. How in the world were you able to lift it?" The answer was, "It had to be done." Lucky for the pilot, the man didn't sit down and analyze, "Let me see, this chopper weighs, say 3000 pounds and I've been to a gym and can dead lift 400, therefore I can't pick this up, but I'll give it a try." The rescuer didn't even consider how much the helicopter weighed; he just picked it up because it had to be done.

Humans have a tendency to over-analyze things and athletes are far worse at this than the general population. Probably the worst among athletes are individual sport athletes who compete against time or a score. This includes your young swimmer. You may have already noticed.

On very rare occasions, a swimmer gets up on the block and swims great because, "It just had to be done." This happens in relays more often than individual races. It is a wonderful thing when swimmers don't think about how fast they have to swim, but just swim fast to get the job done. This type of behavior is more common in younger children because they tend to do less analyzing than their older counterparts and they have a lot farther to go to reach their "potential". Unfortunately, as a swimmer gains more experience, these spontaneous great swims happen less often. That's when another avenue for improvement must be found.

True Expectations

There is an overriding basis for all athletic performances once athletes have become familiar with competition. Since this book is about swimming, this is really saying that there is an overriding basis for *swimming* performances once *swimmers* have completed a few consistent races. It isn't their level of conditioning. Neither is it their physical strength. The true basis for swimming performance is *belief*—what swimmers believe they can swim—their *"true expectations"*. Swimmers stand behind the starting blocks and negotiate with themselves. At the end of their negotiations, without even knowing it, they have determined what time they will swim. The truth is, swimmers are negotiating with themselves long before they *get* to the swim meet. They do it in practice, they do it before they sleep, and they do it when they're in school daydreaming. Then, during the race, after the starting horn sounds, they go out and swim it. The secret to enhancing swimmers' performances isn't to strengthen or condition them, though these help affect the *true* key. The secret to enhancing swimmers' performances is to change their true expectations of how fast they are.

True expectations are what swimmers are confident they can do, deep down inside. They are not goals or hopes or dreams. Swimmers may comment that they would like to swim a certain time in a meet. This is not a true expectation. It is a goal or a desire. Ninety-nine percent of the time, goals are not true expectations. True expectations are based upon an individual's self-confidence in a particular situation, in our case, a swimming race (what Albert Bandura, 1977, 1982 calls self-efficacy).

True expectations come from *somewhere* and they are constantly being affected and changed. Affecting change in swimmers' true expectations is the key to enhancing their performances. The following sections will shed light on how swimmers get their true expectations and how those expectations can be changed.

Past Performances

True expectations are based on a number of things. Primary among them is past performance—Swimmers who have swum a certain distance in 30 seconds, likely feel they can swim it in 30 seconds again. This is a pretty simple concept and it forms the backbone of a swimmer's true expectations. But if it were the only thing that helped form true expectations, then swimmers would rarely get personal best times because they would only have confidence they could do what they had already done. Since personal bests are common, especially in young age groups, there is obviously more than this basic principle to the formation of true expectations.

Seeing is Believing

In the mid-1900's, sport scientists said the 4-minute mile could not be broken by a human. For several years following this statement, runners heard those words and could not find within themselves the conviction, the confidence (the *true expectation*) that a 4-minute mile *was* possible, for them or even anyone else. On May 6th, 1954, however, Roger Bannister ran a 3:59.4 mile. The following year, several runners (who previously may never have thought it was possible) also broke the 4-minute barrier. Why? Because they saw someone else do it and now knew it *was* possible. For their true expectations to be a sub 4-minute mile, they needed that extra piece of the puzzle of someone else performing it first. In swimming, it is relatively easy for young athletes to drop time because they see so many of their older teammates swimming faster. Teams with a few fast swimmers tend to develop more fast swimmers. This is not necessarily because the coaches are good, but because, if team members are swimming fast, it becomes normal and people tend to gravitate to what is normal and expected. Swimmers see that a time or performance is not impossible and that in fact, if she can do it, then I probably can too.

Of course, there are times when swimmers break world records and, like Roger Bannister, break significant milestones for the first time. These athletes obviously didn't see someone else do it first. In order to achieve this type of performance, these athletes changed their true expectations using other methods. These other methods of changing true expectations are the heart and soul of improvement in not only swimming, but in all sports and many aspects of life.

Rationalization

The first of these methods is rational determination of perform-ance, or rationalization. This happens when swimmers can rationalize improvements based on things they have recently accomplished or changes in physical attributes. For example, if David has worked on his start and now believes his start is faster and can gain him half a second, his true expectation of an upcoming 50 freestyle performance will be a half second faster. Perhaps Sarah swam 59 seconds in a 100 freestyle race, but during the race, her feet slipped off a turn. Sarah would rationalize that if she swam the race with a non-slip turn, she would improve her time. Hence, the next time she swims the race, she will expect a time faster than she swam before. If David grew taller and stronger since the last time he raced, he might assume these physical changes would lead to faster times. These kinds of rationali-zation come easily early in swimming. It can take several years before young swimmers swim races without making some kind of physical error which can be corrected and young swimmers are growing rap-idly.

Improvements based on rationalization are really changes in true expectations based on physical changes or changes in race strategy. Physical changes are easy for coaches to teach and coaches will spend 90-100% of their time developing physical changes in their swim-mers. This is helpful in the early years of swimming where improve-ment is so heavily physically based (90%). However, as swimmers near their physical potentials, swimming improvement becomes more and more mental. With this and growing children in mind, the next three ways to change true expectations are mentally, not physically based.

Emotional Arousal

The first of these is arousal. There are two different kinds of arousal; physical and mental, each with internal and external components. Physical arousal is getting the body physically prepared to swim fast which can be accomplished mostly through warm-up. Mental arousal, both internal and external will be somewhat blended together in this discussion and broadly termed "emotional arousal."

Most people have seen how arousal affects athletic performance, either actually at games or on television, when one team comes into a game very "fired-up" and totally dominates the other team, even when that "fired-up" team was not supposed to win. If you've been around swimming long enough, you may have seen best times swum when a swimmer is very excited to swim in a meet. When a swimmer's season is pointing towards a certain meet, that swimmer will place more mental energy towards that meet. In doing this, the swimmer often spends a lot of time *thinking* about swimming fast and this leads to a change in the swimmer's true expectations on the day of the meet.

How is emotional arousal created in a swimmer? In general, it can be done internally or externally. Internal arousal comes from swimmers themselves. There are infinite ways by which swimmers can psych themselves up; probably as many ways as there are swimmers, since no two human's minds work exactly alike. The point is, it comes from within. External sources of arousal are *outside* the swimmers themselves. These sources include coaches, teammates, parents, friends, and other influential individuals, as well as music, movies and anything that has an impact on an individual's motivation and belief.

Can a swimmer experience performance improving emotional arousal at every meet? Not usually. It is possible the swimming system (and other sport's systems) take the emotional arousal out of many meets (or games) by subliminally, and sometimes not subliminally, telling athletes that it's only important how they perform at the culminating meet of the season. In this way, swimmers learn to *"get up"* only a few times a year for *big* meets. This is a shame because if swimmers had swam faster or won more races during the season (perhaps because of increased emotional arousal) they would go into the final *big* meet(s) of the season with better past performances, which would lead to even higher true expectations. In other words, *"It's not bad to swim fast"*.

So then the question is, if some emotional arousal is good, is more arousal better? The answer to that depends on the swimmer. There are some swimmers who completely fall apart with even the smallest amount of emotional arousal. There are some that seem to get better no matter how pumped up they get. Most swimmers fall somewhere between these extremes. It's good to know where your child fits on this pendulum. Most swimmers will follow the inverted U for arousal. As arousal increases, performance increases to a point (the top of the inverted U) after which more arousal decreases performance.

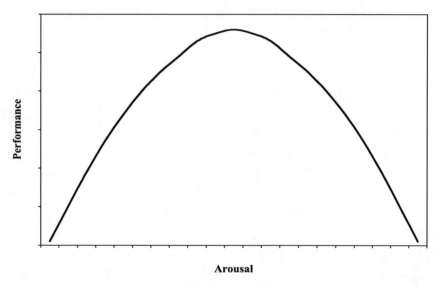

U-shaped curve of performance vs. arousal

There may be as many optimum levels of emotional arousal on a team as there are swimmers. In other words, what arouses one swimmer may not arouse another. Because of this, attempts to arouse swimmers should be done selectively. This flies contrary to the big pep talk for which team sports coaches are famous. This is not to say that swim coaches should not give pep talks to their teams, but they should keep them low key and then work individually with those who perhaps need more arousal. Parents can help or hurt the process depending on how much a coach interacts with their swimmer. If parents know their child swims best with more arousal, they can encourage their child verbally, let them jump around (which would be a combination of mental and physical arousal). If the child needs calming, parents can direct and help that child to sit and visualize the upcoming race, meditate, or just relax. If you think about it, as a parent you are probably already experienced in changing the arousal level in your child.

Be aware, though, of how your child receives any input from you. Your swimmer is your child first and a swimmer second. Children need to know they are loved regardless of performance. A very bad situation arises when children believe (whether true or not), that their parents love them more because they swim fast. Children with siblings in the same sport may think that their parents love the faster swimmer more because they see that swimmer getting more positive attention from the parent. Make sure all of your children get positive strokes independent of their performances. And if need be, leave the arousal control to your child and the coach.

Three Kinds of Motivation

To successfully raise or lower arousal, a swimmer's motivation must be taken into account. In a very general way, swimmers can be divided into three motivational groups: 1) ones who swim well because they need to please, 2) ones who swim well to prove the world wrong, and 3) ones who swim well regardless. When swimmers fall into the last category—those who swim well regardless—leave them alone and they'll be fine. Those in the first category, who swim well because they want to please, *need* positive reinforcement. Positive words, actions, and body language raise the true expectations of these athletes. Negative words and actions towards them or their swimming abilities generally lower their true expectations and performance. Swimmers in the middle category, those who perform well to prove the world wrong, need to be constantly challenged. A comment like, "It would be nice if you could win that race, but Rachel is probably just too fast for you," can inspire an intense desire to perform. These kinds of swimmers usually reveal themselves with comments like, "Hey Mom, do you think I can run to the car and back in ten seconds?" They want the parent to say no, because if the parent says yes, they don't have anything to prove and they like to do things others don't think they can.

The above three categories are general. Some swimmers can be placed in one and only one of these categories. If you have a swimmer that needs to be challenged to perform their best, that may entail a lot of negative comments from your swimmer's coach. Such talk is not usually healthy for a good *parent*-child relationship, but it *can* be healthy for a good *coach*-swimmer relationship and it doesn't mean that the coach doesn't like your child. The coach's job is to develop fast swimmers, just as yours is to love and support your child. Most swimmers don't fit into only one category, however, and there are times for challenges, times for positive reinforcement, and times for letting swimmers do it on their own. In the long run, if swimming is to prepare children for life, they must learn to perform on their own.

Mental Rehearsal

The next mentally based way to change a swimmer's true expectations is called mental rehearsal and is the imagining of a physical process (*mental* practice). Studies of mental rehearsal show two things: 1) performance is improved with mental practice compared to no practice; and 2) mental practice and physical practice together improves performance more than physical practice alone (Weinberg, 1981; Feltz & Landers, 1983). The brain apparently has a hard time distinguishing between mental and physical practice. Strengthening movement patterns in the brain with *mental* practice can cause changes in swimmers' true expectations as much as physical practice. Athletes who learn to mentally rehearse performances early in their swimming careers will have an advantage not only in swimming, but in other life challenges as well.

Mental rehearsal is imagining a future event in detail. In swimming, this generally means an upcoming swimming race, but mental rehearsal can also be used to prepare swimmers for the nervous feeing they might get as their name is introduced and the camera pans on them for the Olympic Trial Finals in the 100 Butterfly.

In general, mental rehearsal will be used to prepare for a swimming race. Here is how it might go for the beginning of a 200 Individual Medley.

Standing behind the blocks, I take two deep breaths before the whistle blows. I step up on the blocks and set my feet. I hear, "Take your marks." I reach down to grab the front of the starting block and I am crouching like a cat ready to pounce. When the beep sounds, I spring up towards the flags. As I reach peak height, I bend at my waist and my hands, followed by my arms, followed by my head and chest, knife into the water. My legs follow in the same hole toes pointed and I shoot forward towards the other end. I start my dolphin kicks, taking four large, powerful kicks followed by three faster ones, followed by three very fast ones and I break out, arms moving forward, taking my first stroke, head down. I keep my stroke long, yet my turnover is quick and I glide on top of the water breathing every other stroke. Three strokes from the wall, I see my turn and slightly adjust my stroke so that I hit the wall with outstretched hands. As my hands touch the wall, I quickly shove my left elbow back towards the other end of the pool, thinking, "Elbow your brother". I move my feet to the wall and move my right hand behind my right ear, thinking, "Phone your mother". My hands come together in a streamline, right hand over left and again I dolphin kick off the wall with the 4, 3, 3 pattern, . .
.

Mental rehearsal in this manner covers most of the important things that swimmers think about going into a race. This kind of practice reinforces the movement patterns in the brain that are associated with the swim very much as does physically swimming the race. And in many cases, good mental rehearsal is *better* than physical practice, because athletes are less likely to make mistakes during a visualized exercise than during real exercise. The saying, "Practice doesn't make perfect, *perfect* practice makes perfect," is very accurate. Once swimmers are confident that they can perform a race with improved technique and without errors (because they have visualized themselves doing so) increased true expectations will move them towards faster performances.

Self-Talk

Self-talk can be defined as the things we communicate to ourselves either verbally or in thought. These conversations with ourselves affect what we feel and believe. Learning to control self-talk can greatly enhance swimmers' true expectations. The conversations humans have with themselves can be positive, neutral or negative. If self-talk is negative, we often call it self-defeating. If it is positive, it can provide a great boost in confidence and ultimately, in performance.

By the time children become swimmers, they are already self-talkers. Stand around the pool deck and you can hear it. "Why is Suzy in all my races? She always wins!" If this swimmer expresses these thoughts out loud, how many times has she said them silently to herself using self-talk? The good thing is that age-group swimmers are still young enough for parents to influence their self-talk.

Parents can and should teach self-talk to their children. The first step is to find out how children currently talk to themselves. Ask your young swimmers what they say to themselves before practice or a race. Then listen very carefully to both their verbal and non-verbal answers. You might find your child has positive self-talk before one race and negative self-talk before another (a different stroke or distance) or before practice. If a child seems to have positive self-talk, good! If a child has negative or even neutral self-talk, try introducing some new self-talk thoughts. The goal is to go from, "I don't think I can," to "I think I can," to "I can!" Here are some examples of negative thoughts and some suggestions to turn a swimmer's self-talk to the positive side.

Self-talk for practices:

(Negative) I don't feel good today. I'll just ease back. It won't matter, I'll feel better tomorrow and then I'll go hard.
(Positive) I've felt better, but these are the days that can make me great. I'll prove to myself that I'm good even when I don't feel my best.

(Neg) I hate this workout—the coach never writes workouts that I like.
(Pos) The coach is writing workouts that will benefit the whole team, me included. If I'd like something a little different I'll talk to the coach later.

(Neg) I'm hurting; I can't stay up for the rest of the swim.
(Pos) I've felt better, but I'll be hurting like this in any race. This is a chance to make a gain. I'll focus on making one perfect stroke at a time.

(Neg) I'll ease into this set and just swim the last *repeat hard. After all, I don't know what the coach has planned for the next set.*
(Pos) I need to challenge myself on this set and that means laying it on the line before *the last couple repeats and then giving it everything to hold my pace. That's the way I'll improve.*

(Neg) I'm not sure if I'll reach my goals at the championship meet.

(Pos) I can best meet my goals if I continue to strive to perform in practice. I will do the things in practice every day to meet those goals. When I get to the championship meet I'll be ready.

Self talk for races:

(Neg) I'm not sure if I'm faster than these swimmers or not.

(Pos) It doesn't matter how fast the other swimmers are. I can't control them, but I can *control myself! I'm going to do my very best.*

(Neg) She's pulling away from me.

(Pos) Stay calm; I've got a plan for how I'll swim my best, stick with it. I've come from behind before—just stay efficient.

(Neg) I'm not as fast as Ian on the start. How can I stay with him?

(Pos) I will make my start as good as possible by being streamlined and I'll make up the difference in other parts of the swim—I want it more than he does and in the end, that will be the difference.

Parents can change their swimmer's self-talk by identifying negative self-talk and verbally changing the thought to a positive one. To reinforce the positive self-talk, parents should have their swimmer repeat the new thought several times. Eventually, the idea is to train swimmers to identify their *own* self-talk and when it is negative, change it to positive. This technique can be used in all areas of a child's life, not just around the pool.

Self-fulfilling Prophecy

The last technique I will discuss to help swimmers change their true expectations is the use of the Self-fulfilling Prophecy. In 1968, two researchers, Rosenthal and Jacobson discovered an interesting psychological aspect of humans when they told some teachers that a few of the students in their classes were "intellectual late bloomers", meaning they should soon be blossoming intellectually. Hearing this information, the teachers began to expect more from these students and in doing so, began to *treat* them with high expectations. The children's tests scores rose significantly over their classmates' scores to the point where they *became* the intellectual late bloomers that the researchers predicted. The only thing was that these children had *not* been tagged by tests as "late bloomers", but had tested in the average range. What this showed the researchers was that humans tend to fulfill the expectations of those around them.

The Self-fulfilling Prophecy is critical in developing swimmers and one of the key concepts covered in this book. Athletes are like the young school students in the study. They pick up on everything that a coach/parent/teacher says and does. They notice the tone of voice and the eye contact. They read body language and see how the coach/parent/teacher talks with other athletes/siblings/students. They get placed in a pecking order. They soon do what is expected of them. They become what the coach's/parent's/teacher's prophecy is for them. And saying, "I expect all of you to always try your best," while helpful, will not override unconscious body language and attention or lack thereof to the contrary. It is commonly thought that 70% of all communication is non-verbal and that certainly applies here.

Self-fulfilling Prophecy can be helpful or harmful depending on the expectation. Remember from earlier, the body is strong but the mind is weak. A vast majority of swimmers have the potential to become great because their *bodies* are capable, but early in their swimming careers they get tagged as "average" and they develop to fulfill those expectations. One of the most difficult things for a coach to do is to treat each swimmer like they have great potential. Even though a swimmer may not be swimming fast today, the coach and parents should treat the swimmer as if someday soon, that swimmer will become quite good indeed—a *swimming* "late bloomer". Both coach and parent should be really excited about the swimmer's potential. For a coach, it's not hard to do this when working with maybe 10 swimmers. However, when there are 50 or more athletes to deal with, there is very little time for a coach to make contact with each one. The "average" swimmer is left to think they *are* average and to read subtle signs from the coach. This is the way it is and probably the way it will always be. Coaches mainly coach the physical aspects of swimming, which are easy and definable. In doing this, they let the mentally strong among their swimmers sort themselves out. Don't blame them. With 50+ kids per coach, it's all there is time for.

As a parent, the mental training of the Self-fulfilling Prophecy falls upon you. A great majority of parents mentally train their children, often without even realizing it. Think about it. We parents are continually working to get our children to perform their best in everything they do—schoolwork, sports, manners, the list goes on. We are constantly trying to gain insight into our children's thought processes so we can improve our children. That is the job of a parent. But for a parent to change a child's mental outlook towards swimming it takes far more than just saying, "You look like you're swimming well today." If a parent rarely comments on a child's swimming, this statement may have a positive effect. However, it will be ignored if used too many times. Here's where education on the finer points of swimming can enable parents to comment on various aspects of a child's performance and practice (Chapters 4 & 5). Now, there is a fine line between comments that show caring and spur on motivation and those that cause pressure that kill motivation. Children will send out clues as to where they are if you pay attention. If they are listening to your comments and they seek your feedback, good for you. If they seem to be ignoring you or start shutting down, you need to change tactics.

Remember, the Self-fulfilling Prophecy is more than just words, it's looks and body language and the way you act around others. Little ears may not listen very well when you tell them to set the table or turn off the TV, but they catch everything when you're talking about them to your friends. How you act and what you say is highly individual to the situation and the child involved. Here are some good comments.

"Wow, when you streamline off your turns, you look really fast." A comment like this reinforces that they *should* streamline off their turns and that when they do streamline, they are fast, perhaps faster than the other swimmers. So, from now on when they streamline, they will feel like they can swim faster. This will change their true expectations (as well as improve their streamlines).

"Your start looks really good. When your feet follow your hands through the same hole, you look like you've been shot from a cannon." Again, you are reinforcing a positive swimming behavior. The fact that you noticed their start and commented on how fast it got them traveling in the water makes them think they do it better than others. This will give them confidence which in turn will raise their true expectations.

Here's another one—a friend or perhaps a relative watches a child swim. If the guest makes a very direct comment about the child's swimming (perhaps requested to by the parent), that statement may have a great impact. "I was watching your butterfly and you look very powerful. I could see how much more power you have than the other kids in the pool." By the way, if the child has good technique in butterfly and average power, this comment could make that child *feel* very strong in the butterfly stroke. The next day in practice, the child may remember that comment when swimming butterfly and work a bit harder during a set. The harder work will *make* the child stronger and the prophecy will be fulfilled.

In the examples above, a parent must know enough about swimming to make intelligent comments that reinforce what's being coached. The next few chapters in the book will help you learn a number of things about swimming, well beyond what your child knows. This will make your comments more effective. Working the Self-fulfilling Prophecy is not a quick fix to drop times. Nothing in this book is. The Self-fulfilling Prophecy is a life-long approach to excellence that parents can selectively use in many aspects of their children's development.

I have written this chapter (and book) for parents, but parents must understand that the coach has more clout for swimming matters in a child's mind than the parent ever can and that's the way it *should* be. Hopefully, your child's coach exhibits high expectations for all the swimmers on the team.

Mental Strength Wrap-up

I purposely placed this mental chapter early in the book because of its importance. Much of the rest of the book goes into the physical aspects of swimming. Because I have devoted more chapters to the physical aspects of swimming, please don't fall into the trap of thinking the physical aspects are more important than the mental ones. This could not be farther from the truth. There are those who think swimming is one of, if not *the* most physically demanding of all sports. Swimming workouts are certainly physically demanding. However, performance in most swimming races (anything 200 meters and shorter) is oriented much more around *skill* than endurance or muscular strength. Being skilled in an event represents a defined motor pattern. Motor patterns are stored in and executed by the brain. When swimmers stand on the blocks, the desire to win comes from their brains (not their bodies). Their belief that they can win comes from their brains too (not their bodies). The motor pattern skills, the desire to perform and the belief that one can win separate the champions from the pack. You, the parent, can shape each of these qualities.

This shaping can be done every day in everything you do and say to your child. Don't stop reading the book, but you now know the most important secret to swimming success. Superior *mental* strength, not physical strength is what really separates the champions. This does not mean the physical aspects of swimming are not important. The physical elements of swimming supplement the mental, so read on.

THREE

THE FLEXIBLE SWIMMER

Stretching is a very misunderstood concept in sports. If you are a runner who stretches your calf muscles prior to a run, you are an individual who probably misunderstands stretching. This includes most of us because it is more habitual than anything else. Think about stretching using this exaggerated analogy, roll some clay into a long cylinder and put it in the refrigerator. After some time, take it out and pull both ends. It doesn't take long for the middle to tear. Now, if you were to have warmed that clay up, then you would have been able to stretch it perhaps twice as far before a tear occurred. Muscles are material, and like clay, warm muscles can stretch further without tearing than cold muscles can.

Studies have supported this, showing that passive muscle stretching *before* exercise not only increases the chance of injury, but lowers the amount of power a muscle can produce after the stretch (Cornwell et al., 2002; Nelson & Kokkonen, 2001). Most people stretch prior to exercise because they believe that it will prevent injury during exercise and soreness afterwards. Much research on this subject has been completed over the past few years, however, and the evidence does not support either assumption (Herbert & Gabriel, 2002; Whitfield, 2002). So what does this mean—don't stretch, chapter over? Not at all. Flexibility is very important to a swimmer, both for proper stroke form and for increased overall hydrodynamics (ease of the body moving through the water).

Since this book is about your child, how about flexibility in children? Most children are naturally flexible by adult standards. Some are extremely flexible and there *is* a limit to how much flexibility is good for an athlete. Athletes who have too much flexibly can be prone to injury just as those who are not flexible enough. Flexibility *is* a good thing, but too much of a good thing is often bad.

Before describing what body parts need to be flexible and how swimmers can get that flexibility, it must be noted that every swimmer is different and the amount of flexibility each can obtain is unique to that swimmer alone. The stretches and exercises detailed in this chapter will suit most swimmers, but not *every* swimmer. Before you have your child attempt any of the stretches diagramed in this book you may wish to consult a medical professional with respect to the health of your child's joints and muscles.

So what have I said so far? "Don't stretch" and "Flexibility is both good and bad." Confused? Bear with me and I'll explain the ins and outs of flexibility with respect to swimming.

This chapter will cover two kinds of flexibility; joint flexibility and muscle flexibility. The first allows the body to get into a streamlined position. The second allows full range of motion through stroke or kick movements. Before I describe how to increase flexibility in the joints and muscles, a very short discussion of human anatomy will help most readers get on the same page.

The structural support system of the human body is made up of *bones*. Bones don't have the ability to move on their own. To do that, humans need *muscles*. Muscles aren't directly connected to bone. As the muscle gets closer to the bone it changes to become more like bone. This area between the muscle and the bone is called the *tendon*—tendons connect muscles to bones. When swimmers want to increase muscle flexibility, they must increase both muscle *and* tendon flexibility.

Muscles often help with joint stability, but neither they nor tendons are responsible for connecting one bone to another to make a "joint". *Ligaments* connect bones to other bones. Ligaments are very strong tissues, but have much lower nutrient supplies than do muscles. This variance in vascularization (blood flow) is an important fact when trying to increase flexibility.

Flexibility is increased by introducing stress to body tissues—stretching an area enough to cause a lengthening change. Tissues that are stressed by stretching will adapt (become more flexible or longer). Blood helps muscles, tendons and ligaments adapt by bringing nutrients to those tissues. Muscles adapt more quickly than ligaments because of their greater blood flow, hence muscle flexibility is much easier and faster to obtain than is joint flexibility, as joints are comprised mostly of ligaments.

The Ankle Joint

The laws of aerodynamics would indicate that ankle joint flexibility (the ability to point the feet/toes) is vital for swimmers. There are two reasons for this: 1) streamline, and 2) propulsion from the kick. Streamline is of the utmost importance to fast swimming as it reduces drag. The most significant part of the body to *reduce* a swimmer's drag is the feet, and the ability to point the feet requires flexible ankles. Think of a swimmer as a tear drop of water—one of nature's most aerodynamic shapes.

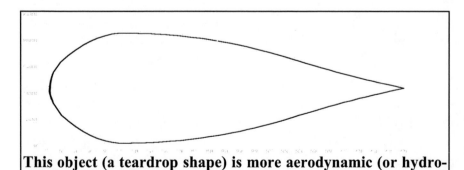

This object (a teardrop shape) is more aerodynamic (or hydrodynamic) going from right to left, than left to right.

A teardrop has a large rounded surface area at the leading end (closest to the Earth as it is falling) and a very small, tapered surface area at the trailing end. A swimmer's body should mimic this shape as it moves through the water—larger front, tapered end. The front end is the head and shoulders while the tapered end should be the feet—if the swimmer has flexible ankles.

What is good ankle flexibility? Here is a test you swimmer can take. Swimmers should be able to sit on the floor with their legs straight out in front of them, and without bending their knees, touch their toes to the ground.

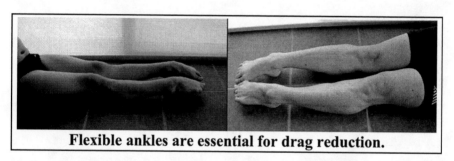

Flexible ankles are essential for drag reduction.

This ankle mobility allows swimmers to have pointed toes while swimming without forcefully using their calf muscles. Swimmers who do not have flexible ankles must either maintain a less than optimal streamline toe-point (poor choice, lots of drag) or use calf muscles while they swim for the sole purpose of pointing their feet to reduce drag. Any extraneous muscle use reduces the total energy available for propulsion, as well as eventually reducing the force available for pushing off a wall (since some of the muscles swimmers use to point their toes are also responsible for push-offs). Also, using muscles to actively point the feet can make swimmers' legs or feet cramp. Having flexible ankles reduces the need for muscles to be highly contracted to maintain a streamlined position.

The other benefit of flexible ankles is an increase in the potential force that kicking can produce. A flexible ankle is in a much better position to push water than a non-flexible ankle.

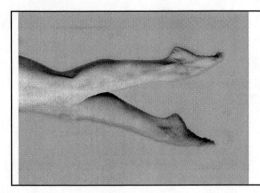

The flexible ankle in both dolphin kicking and flutter kicking (shown) puts the foot at a much better angle to propel the swimmer forward.

Swimmers with non-flexible ankles often flex their *knees* at too great an angle in attempts to gain a better foot position on the water for kicking. The problem with doing this is that greater knee flexion leads to additional drag and slower swimming. Ankle flexibility is basic to fast swimming. Anyone who has been to a swimming meet can see the advantage that a swimmer with a great kick has over the rest of the field. By the way, I'll say it here that *great kickers are made, not born.* Ankle flexibility coupled with kicking practice (usually hard kicking practice) is the key to being a great kicker and is obtainable by almost every swimmer.

Having said all this, how do swimmers gain ankle flexibility? Swimmers can only do this slowly, over time, by stretching the soft tissue in their ankles. Here are a couple good techniques to stretch the ankles. Swimmers should kneel, with their buttocks resting on their heels/soles of their feet and the tops of their feet against the floor. For individuals without flexible ankles, this will be enough stretch to begin with. For those with a bit more ankle flexibility, the next step is to rock back and lift the knees off the ground. More stretch is applied the higher the knees come off the ground. An additional method for ankle stretching can be accomplished while sitting in a chair. Swimmers can tuck their feet under the chair with their toes curled under. They can do this at the dinner table, even at school!

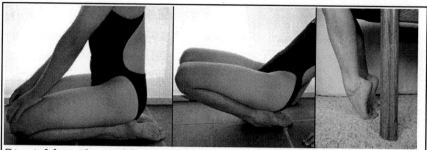

Stretching the ankles is the most important flexibility stretch swimmers can perform. On the left, a swimmer sits on his feet, (middle) rocks back to apply a greater stretch and (right) stretches the ankles in the sitting position with the swimmer's feet under a chair.

How long will it take your swimmer to be able to touch his/her toes to the floor with legs extended out front? That depends on several factors. In general, younger children increase their flexibility quicker than older children. This is why it is important to work on flexibility from the start. Obviously, individuals who are already near touching the floor may get there before those who can't yet make their feet go in a straight line from their legs. But remember what was said earlier about ligaments.

When swimmers stretch their ankles, they are stretching a number of soft tissues including *ligaments*. Ligaments get fewer nutrients from the bloodstream and thus do not respond to stress as rapidly as muscles do. This means two things to the swimmer. First, care should be taken to avoid overstretching the ankle which could damage this important joint. Second, any significant flexibility improvements could take several months. This is a slow process, not a quick fix with the instant gratification of faster swimming times tomorrow. However, it will over the long run reward your swimmer greatly.

Will everyone be able to touch their toes to the ground (as shown earlier) if they work on ankle flexibility for a year? No. There *are* individuals who may not have the genetic make-up to point their feet that far. This doesn't mean they will never be good swimmers or won't get anything out of swimming, but they *are* at a biomechanical (*physical*) disadvantage. This may be grim news to some, but remember that *mental* toughness is far more important to success than anything physical. In addition, stretching the ankles will increase ankle flexibility in *any* swimmer and *any* increase is good because it improves streamline.

I would like to lay out some cautions before parents begin an ankle-stretching program with their children. First, swimmers should not begin actively stretching their ankles if they have a known ankle problem. Parents who have any questions about their child's ankle flexibility or health should see a medical professional before starting their swimmer on any stretching program. Second, flexible ankles, while good for swimming, may not be good for other sports, especially those that require quick cuts like basketball and soccer. Children with *very* flexible ankles stand a greater chance of "rolling" their ankles (though being more flexible, that won't injure them as much as it would someone with a less flexible ankle). Finally, to stress it again, this is a long-term stretching program, not designed to see results in a day or even a week. Time spent in a stretched position is good and swimmers should feel a stretch, but not pain. In this case, swimmers want quantity over quality—do it a lot, but don't press too hard.

There are two other types of ankle flexibility that are important specifically for breaststrokers. One will be noted in the knee section. The other will be discussed in *muscle flexibility*.

The Shoulder Joint

The shoulder joint is the most worked joint in swimming. Shoulder flexibility is important for proper streamline, starts, turns and all four strokes. The shoulder is a somewhat loose-fitting ball and socket joint that allows a wide range of motion. It is also different than the ankle in that stretching of the shoulder joint involves the lengthening of not only ligaments, but several muscles and tendons. Even though shoulder stretches have an effect on all of these tissues, swimmers must increase their flexibility as if they are working solely on ligaments, meaning very slowly, as these are the slowest to conform.

Before going too far into shoulder flexibility, here's a quick warning. The shoulder joint is the most used and often injured joint in swimming. Shoulder stretching for swimmers who already have painful shoulders can increase the pain and prolong recovery time (McMaster & Troup, 1993). Swimmers already experiencing shoulder pain need to be very careful if they stretch so that they do not further aggravate injury. On the other hand, shoulder flexibility or lack thereof does not seem to be a contributing factor in shoulder pain (Bak & Magnusson, 1997). So don't think your swimmer will be more prone to a shoulder injury because he/she has or develops flexible shoulders.

The shoulder joints need to be flexible enough to obtain a proper streamline position. This streamline position starts with one hand over the other with the arms fully extended overhead, pressing against the ears. When standing swimmers attempt to get their arms into this position, they should form a straight line from their fingertips to their ankles. This position is necessary as a minimum. Increased flexibility in this position can greatly increase the velocity swimmers transfer from the air into the water during a start and off the wall after a turn push-off.

A lack of shoulder flexibility, specifically the ability to articulate the arms in a plane behind the back, makes the stroke of butterfly in particular very difficult. As a swimming spectator, you may have seen swimmers who have trouble getting their arms out of the water while performing butterfly. Lack of shoulder flexibility may be compensated for in freestyle and backstroke with greater body rotation, but not in butterfly where the arms must recover over the water simultaneously. There is no way to be a great *butterflier* without adequate shoulder flexibility. And swimmers of the other three strokes place themselves at a disadvantage if they do not posses flexible shoulders as well.

Shoulder flexibility to the back can be increased with the help of a fellow swimmer (when children are younger, this is best accomplished by an adult).

Another addition to shoulder flexibility is what is often called "hyperextension" of the shoulders during streamlines and the forward-most reaching part of each stroke. This motion allows swimmers to lengthen their bodies from head to toe, which reduces drag. "Hyperextending" the shoulders during the forward-most part of all four strokes not only reduces drag by making the body longer and thinner, but increases the length of every underwater arm pull.

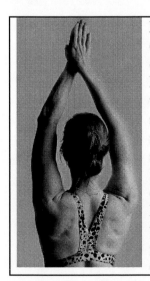
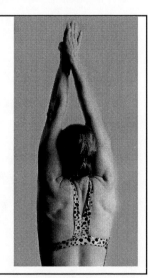

Normal streamline (left) vs. "hyperextended" streamline (right). Note the narrower shoulders and the smaller triangular space above the head in the "hyperextended" position. Minor changes like this can mean a great deal of difference in the water.

Now that some benefits of shoulder flexibility have been explained, the question is, how do swimmers increase their shoulder flexibility? The answer again is, slowly. Ligaments are involved. There are several different stretches that can be applied.

To stretch the shoulders overhead, swimmers stand in the streamline position and lean forward against a wall. Those who can extend their shoulders more than 20° beyond the 180° streamline position from hips to hands (by pressing the chest down) probably have enough shoulder flexibility and should stretch only to maintain, not to increase it.

Working the streamline position against a wall is one of the best ways to increase streamline in the water for all strokes, starts and turns.

To stretch the shoulders out to the *side*, place one hand on the wall at shoulder level and rotate away from it (so the arm is pressed to the rear). In this stretch swimmers feel like they are pushing the wall around themselves.

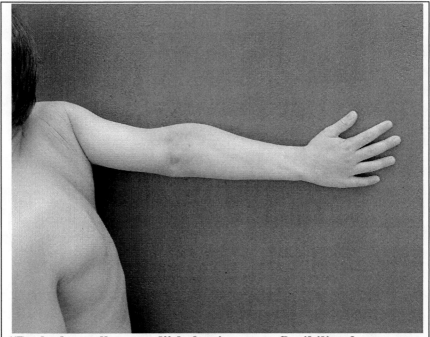

"Push the wall around" helps increase flexibility for arm recovery during butterfly and freestyle and can place the hand in a better pull position for backstroke.

Another way to accomplish this stretch is with a partner. The partner can take both hands at the same time, keeping them at shoulder level or slightly lower and bring them gently towards each other behind the swimmer's back. Swimmers whose hands touch easily behind their backs are flexible enough in this direction. Some swimmers may be able to cross their arms all the way to their elbows. It is unclear whether this additional amount of flexibility is helpful during swimming.

Other stretching exercises to increase shoulder flexibility include the pole or towel stretch. In this stretch, swimmers grasp a towel or pole with both hands and, without bending their elbows, rotate the pole from the front of their bodies overhead to the back and then forward again. As shoulder flexibility increases, the hands are moved closer together on the pole or towel. The goal should be to do the exercise with the hands slightly more than shoulder width apart. If swimmers use a solid object, like a pole or PVC pipe for this stretch, they can motivate themselves by marking their progress as their hands get closer to the center on the pole or pipe.

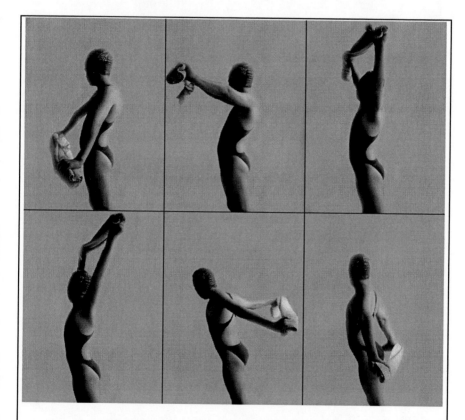

A shoulder stretch using a towel or rod can quickly increase shoulder flexibility, which will improve a swimmer's freestyle, backstroke and butterfly.

To help increase shoulder "hyperextension" overhead, swimmers can hang from a pull-up bar while trying to relax the shoulders. This is very good for streamline flexibility.

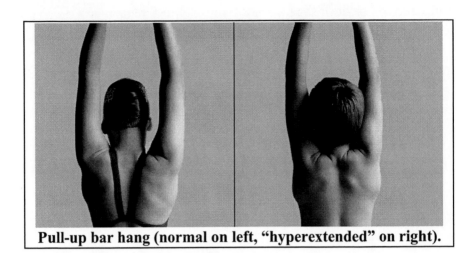

Pull-up bar hang (normal on left, "hyperextended" on right).

To increase shoulder flexibility in the *back* of the shoulder, pull the elbow of a straight arm across the chest towards the opposite shoulder.

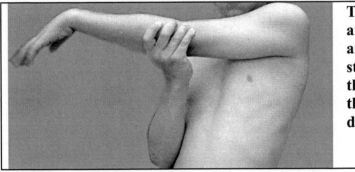

The front arm pull is an effective stretch for the back of the shoulders.

This stretch can help with the streamline position but is mostly important to help balance the flexibility in the shoulders. If the arm can be easily pulled to the chest without discomfort, a swimmer has enough flexibility of the shoulder in this plane of motion and should just lightly stretch to maintain that flexibility.

Another good shoulder exercise is a backbend. To stretch in a backbend, swimmers should get into a backbend position and hold it for at least 20 seconds. As swimmers become more flexible, the hands and feet can come closer together. The idea is to concentrate on extending the shoulders as well as the back.

The backbend can help both shoulder and back flexibility. The key to helping both back and shoulder flexibility is to extend the elbows when performing the backbend.

There are many variations of shoulder stretches that can help increase shoulder joint flexibility. If a different variation seems to be more suited for your swimmer, you may want to try that one. Again, I will print a word of caution. Swimmers should not begin stretching their shoulders if they have a shoulder problem. If parents have any questions about their child's shoulders, they should see a medical professional. No two swimmers are alike and the flexibility optimums I have expressed above are examples of what *can* be done, not what each swimmer *must* do. Finally, this is a long term stretching program, not designed to see results in a day or even a week. You want *quantity* over quality—swimmers need to do a lot of conservative stretching rather than *over*-stretching in hopes of faster improvement.

The Knee Joint

The knee is an interesting joint and is usually not a flexibility concern to freestylers, backstrokers or butterfliers. However, it *is* a concern to breaststrokers. Knees were designed to flex and extend in one plane of motion, back to front. Breaststroke requires *lateral* (side to side) flexibility. As this is not natural, many swimmers are not flexible in this way, and because they are not, may struggle with breaststroke. But, with persistence and breaststroke mileage, their knees *will* become more flexible. There is a way to stretch both the knees and ankles for breaststroke at the same time. Swimmers kneel on the floor, bottom on the ground and ankles to either side of their hips, arches down, in a "W" stretch. If their knees and ankles are flexible enough, their feet can be pointed outward with the insides of their anklebones touching the ground. Until that point, toes should remain tucked under to put less pressure on the knees.

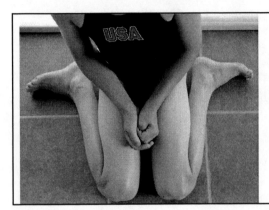

Left is the leg position for the "W" breaststroke stretch. Be careful with this stretch as it tends to place a lot of unnatural stress on the knees.

This knee and ankle stretch can be very uncomfortable if the swimmer is not flexible in either the knees or the ankles. In addition, some may experience hip pain when performing this stretch. If this occurs (as with any stretch), a medical evaluation should be performed before continuing. Like all the stretches covered so far, the "W' stretch should be attempted slowly and progress made should be measured in months, not days.

The Back

Flexibility of the back can be an advantage in swimming. Swimmers can more easily obtain and maintain a streamlined position on starts and turns if their backs are flexible. Back flexibility can also help rotation during freestyle and backstroke. A flexible back is important for proper starts, whether front entry or backstroke as well as body position in all four strokes.

The back is made up of 25 vertebrae. These joints allow the back to extend, flex and twist along almost its entire length. One of the best ways to gain or keep flexibility in the back is to stretch in the back-bend position detailed earlier. The backbend should be held for at least 20 seconds, lie back down and repeat. Back flexibility can be measured as swimmers' hands get closer to their feet. A stretch for the *lower* back is the "knee to floor" stretch. Swimmers start this stretch by lying on their backs with one hip flexed 90°. The opposite hand then pulls the knee to the floor. This stretch is done on both sides.

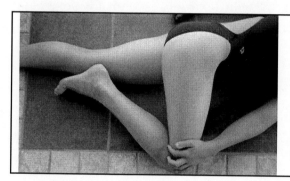

The "Knee to Floor" back stretch will help increase lower back flexibility. This is especially helpful in backstroke and freestyle.

Muscle Stretching

Muscle flexibility is important to swimming streamline and possibly increased force production. I want to make sure every reader understands the statement I made at the beginning of this chapter. Stretching cold muscles is more likely to *cause* injury than to prevent it. Swimmers *should* stretch their muscles, but to increase their flexibility, not to prevent injury. And they should only stretch *after* muscles have been warmed up.

In order to gain muscle flexibility, swimmers must stretch, but muscles should be stretched when they are warm. Thus the best time to stretch muscles is *after*, not before a workout. Before a workout, swimmers should do little more than activate their muscles by swinging their arms around in circles and back and forth. They should warm-up in the water, starting slowly for the first few hundred meters of workout—this is why that portion of practice is *called* "warm-up." Following warm-up, swimmers can stretch to work on increasing their flexibility.

Muscles, like joints, *can* become *too* flexible, and in the case of muscles, too much flexibility may reduce their ability to provide support. When this happens, the muscles and the joints they help support may become more prone to injury. Normal stretching exercises, however, while children are training and competing in swimming on a regular basis, are unlikely to make muscles too flexible. If you are worried about how much muscle flexibility is right for your child, consult a physical therapist or a medical professional specializing in swimming.

Upper Body Muscle Stretches

The muscles of the forearm are not often stretched unless athletes are experiencing pain from tight or sore muscles. Forearm muscle flexibility is not a key element in swimming. But, since swimmers often experience tight forearms, here are a couple of easy stretches. To stretch the muscles on the top of the forearm, place the back of the hand on a wall and lower the shoulder (arm straight) until a stretch is felt.

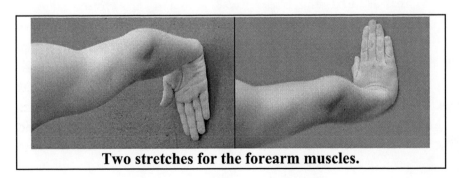

Two stretches for the forearm muscles.

For the muscles on the underside of the forearm, place the *palm* on the wall and slide it down until a stretch is felt. The stretches are held for at least 20 seconds each on both arms.

The triceps muscles (back of the upper arm) are one of the primary propulsive muscle groups in swimming and should be kept flexible for optimal power. To stretch the triceps, place an elbow directly behind the head with the hand touching the back. The opposite hand then grabs the elbow and gently pulls. The stretch should be held for at least 20 seconds on each arm.

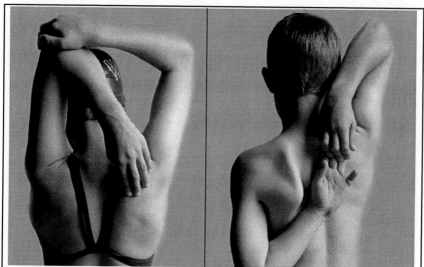

The triceps stretch can be done by pulling across an elbow or by linking the hands together behind the back and pulling.

Another major muscle of the upper body is the latissimus dorsi, often referred to as the lats, which is located below and behind the armpit. All swimming strokes use the lat muscles and the size of a swimmer's lats are usually proportional to how long that athlete has been swimming. To stretch the lats, swimmers should get themselves into a streamline position (stretching the arms overhead) and bend their upper bodies to one side then the other. Hold the stretch for at least 20 seconds on each side.

To the left is an easy way to stretch the latissimus dorsi muscles. This stretch is done on both sides.

The last of the upper body muscles this book will cover are the pectoral muscles. The pectorals are the major muscles of the upper chest. The stretch, "Pushing the wall around" already stretched these muscles.

Another good stretch for the pectorals is sitting with both palms flat on the floor behind the swimmer shoulder-width apart, fingers pointed backwards. With elbows locked, swimmers scoot their bottoms forward or their hands backward. Hold the stretch for at least 20 seconds. There are other stretches that may work the pectoral muscles better, but this stretch performs double duty for the pectorals and the shoulder joints.

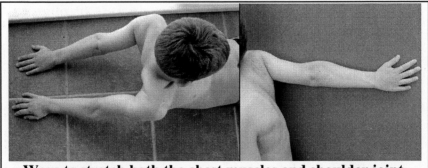

Ways to stretch both the chest muscles and shoulder joint.

Lower Body Muscle Stretches

Proper breaststroke kicking technique requires flexibility in both joints and muscles. In order to get the feet in the proper kicking position for the breaststroke whip kick, swimmers must have flexible calf muscles. Stretching the calf muscles helps in getting more power out of a breaststroke kick. Additionally, it has been shown that people who can dorsiflex their ankles well (bring their toes closer to their shins) are less likely to have ankle injuries. (Tabrizi et al., 2000).

There are two major lower leg muscles in the back of the leg and the following stretches isolate both. For the first stretch, lean against a wall with the leg to be stretched *straight* and behind the body, ankle flexed. The other leg provides balance with the knee bent under the chest. The second stretch is the same but with the knee of the back leg *bent*. These two stretches should be held for at least 20 seconds on each leg.

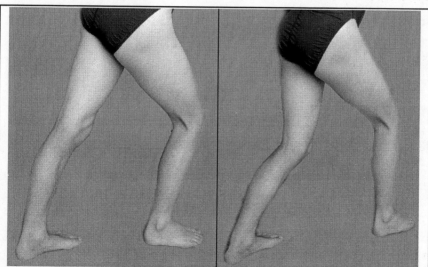

The gastroc stretch (the main calf) is on the left. The soleus stretch (a deeper muscle) is on the right.

The largest muscles in the body are found in the front of the upper legs and are called the quadriceps, or quads. Swimmers who sit on their ankles doing the ankle stretch are also stretching their quads. To stretch the quads even more, swimmers can lean back and even completely *lay* back while they are sitting on their feet. Another way to stretch the quads is to stand near a wall with one hand on the wall for balance and reach with the other hand to grab a foot and pull it up to the buttock. This can be done by grabbing the leg on the same side—right hand to right leg, or by crossing over, right hand to left leg (which provides a slightly better quad stretch). Hold the stretch for at least 20 seconds for each leg.

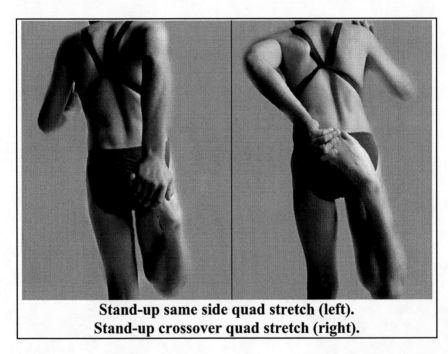

Stand-up same side quad stretch (left).
Stand-up crossover quad stretch (right).

The hamstrings (the back of the upper leg) are famous for tightening up in runners, but they can do the same in swimmers. There are several ways to stretch the hamstrings. Swimmers can sit with one leg straight out in front, the other bent at the knee, foot alongside the buttock. Swimmers then bend forward and reach for their toes. This stretch can be made more effective by doing it repeatedly with different foot positions, once with the foot rotated inward, another time with the foot straight and once with the foot rotated outward. This stretch should be held for at least 20 seconds in each position for each leg, the goal, to touch the chest to the thighs.

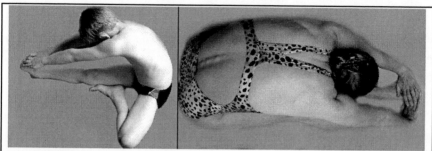

A traditional hamstring stretch (left) has one leg to the side with the leg to be stretched forward, knee straight. The hamstrings should be flexible enough so that swimmers can touch their chests to their legs (right).

The final muscles that will be discussed are those around the groin. This is mainly for breaststroke. The stretch for this is commonly called the butterfly stretch (not the breaststroke stretch) because the legs form the shape of a butterfly. To perform this stretch, sit on the ground and bring the feet together, sole to sole. Then pull the feet within a few inches of the groin and gently press down on the knees with the elbows or hands. The stretch should be held for at least 20 seconds. Flexible swimmers will be able to get their knees within an inch or two of the floor.

The Butterfly Stretch helps keep the groin muscles flexible which is important when training a lot of breaststroke.

It is important to note that all swimmers are different and there may be other stretches that better suit your swimmer. There are a number of good stretching books on the market (though I don't know of any that are specific to swimming). Also, swimmers will find their own flexibility limits. A swimmer should not be pushed towards a non-achievable stretching goal. Everyone can gain from stretching, but what is gained is dependent on the body of the individual doing the stretching.

Stretching doesn't have to be a solo enterprise, either. Almost everyone can profit from being more flexible, so do it together. Dad's can stretch with their kids, Moms can do it, and siblings can do it. Stretching can be a family routine from which everyone will benefit. But remember to warm up, since warm muscles and joints react better to the stress.

FOUR

THE TECHNICAL SWIMMER

Swimming can seem like a very complicated sport everything considered. There are four competitive strokes, and various distance races for each of them. Each stroke has timing, coordination and strength aspects specific to itself. And if all that isn't enough, there is the element of water, which limits the opportunity to breathe. This chapter is not meant to make the reader a biomechanical expert in swimming. It has been written to give parents a foundation so that they can be educated observers of their children, understanding the forces that speed swimmers up and slow them down in the water.

It may sound, from the previous paragraph, that swimming is very complicated (I have certainly painted that picture). But actually, swimming fast *should* be very simple because there are only two things swimmers can do to travel faster through the water: 1) produce more *propulsive force,* and 2) reduce *drag.* For those who like to see things written in equations, here's the "swimming equation":

$$(\text{Swimming Speed})^2 = \frac{2*\text{Drag}}{C_D * S_{wet} * D_w}$$

C_D is the coefficient of drag (how streamlined an object is).
S_{wet} is the surface area of the body touching the water.
D_w is the density of the water.

This may not *look* very simple, but it can essentially be reduced to this.

$$(\text{Swimming Speed})^2 = \text{Drag}$$

The above equation is a very simple and effective way to think about swimming. If swimming speed is one unit, drag is one unit. But when swimming speed is two units, then drag becomes four units. If swimming speed goes to four units, drag increases to 16 units. The only way a swimmer can combat this exponential increase in drag is to lower their C_D (coefficient of drag) by becoming more streamlined. So, the next time you're at a meet and think that a certain swimmer won a race because he or she was bigger and stronger than the rest of the field, think again. Someone who couldn't produce as much force, but who produced less drag could easily have beaten that swimmer.

In the previous chapter, I talked about the flexibility issues affecting drag. Seeing this equation may make it easier to understand why flexible feet and shoulders are so important in swimming—because they *reduce* drag. But what exactly *is* drag and what is *propulsive force* since these two things seem to be the keys to swimming fast. Swimming *drag* is the resistance created when moving a body through the water. If our swimmer Sarah is not moving, then her drag is zero. Once she starts to move, in whatever direction, she begins creating drag and must exert an equivalent force on the water in order to keep moving forward against that drag. *Propulsive force* is simply the combination of forces produced by arms, hands, legs and feet that move the swimmer in the desired direction.

When an individual is swimming at a constant velocity (neither accelerating nor decelerating), drag and propulsive force are equal. Swimmers who increase propulsive force (work harder) will go faster, but their drag will increase until it equals their propulsive force and they are swimming at a faster, but constant velocity again. When swimmers get tired and produce less propulsive force than drag, they will slow down until the drag equals the force they are able to produce.

Now the whole idea behind the sport of swimming is to go fast. In the mindset of a young swimmer, going fast means *working hard,* or producing a lot of propulsive force. There is really nothing wrong with this, but it would be better if swimmers thought, "I need to go fast, I need to make myself more *streamlined."* This is what really makes swimmers fast—decreasing their drag.

Now that we know drag is the true enemy of fast swimming, it's time to talk about how swimmers can reduce it. Drag plagues swimmers during their starts, during their turns and during their strokes. Reducing drag in each of these places is important for fast swimming.

At the start of a swimming race, most swimmers (having entered the water from the starting blocks) are traveling much faster than they can swim. The fastest swimmers can swim at just over two meters per second. Swimmers can enter the water on a start at speeds up to *six* meters per second and then level off in the water before they start stroking at over *three* meters per second (Arata, 1993). They do this by having their upper bodies in a streamlined position and by going through the hole in the water made by their hands. This type of start has been coined the "hole-in-one" start. The hole-in-one start causes much less drag than the opposite extreme, the belly-flop, because less still water is touched (less splash is the clue).

Regarding starts, this seems like a good place to include a short discussion of the two kinds of starts, the traditional 'both feet at the front of the block' start, we'll call the jump-start, and the 'one foot at the front of the block—one foot towards the rear of the block' start known as the track start. If you have been to a swimming meet, you've probably seen both used and may wonder why all swimmers don't use the same one. I would like to quote studies that have analyzed these starts, but no good studies exist so there is no empirical evidence praising one start over the other. Type of start is almost irrelevant for distance swimmers, but most of the best *sprinters* in history have used the jump-start. In recent years, however, many U.S. and Australian swimmers, sprinters as well as distance swimmers have turned to the track start.

Which start is best for your child? In general, swimmers who have powerful jumps and are coordinated *should* do best with the jump-start. This is because the jump-start allows for maximum power from both legs and a center of gravity further forward; the first can translate into greater velocity as swimmers enter the water, while both can translate into a greater distance on entry. Also, children 10 and under may perform better using the jump-start. Many young swimmers using the track start do not get propulsion from their back legs, which contributes to them diving (almost falling) directly into the water. The jump-start gets them up in the air and farther out. If they can then take this jump and develop a hole-in-one entry, they will usually come up with a big lead.

So why are so many people using the track start? One reason may be because it appears that good track starters get off the starting blocks faster. You would think getting of the blocks fast would be good. However, in doing so, these athletes are probably not building up a lot of impulsion (force * time), meaning they will not likely jump as far as a good jump-starter. This impulsion phenomenon was noted in the mid-1900s when comparing different types of track and field starts (Henry, 1952). So getting off the blocks quickly is probably *not* a good reason to use the track start.

There are a number of other reasons why swimmers might use a track start. Swimmers whose legs are extraordinarily long compared to their upper-bodies can have a difficult time springing out of a jump-start position and producing a lot of force, so the track start might be best for them. The track start also offers a very stable position on the starting blocks and since there is a no false start rule in swimming (one false start disqualifies the swimmer from the race), some might use it for security. In addition, many swimmers without good vertical leaps seem to prefer the track start because they don't push-off well from both legs at once. Yet another reason could be that young swimmers see good swimmers using it. The first two swimmers of notability who used a track start were Olympic Gold Medalists and World Record Holders Rowdy Gaines and Mary T. Meagher in the early 1980's. These were two great swimmers and when young swimmers see some of their idols doing something, they change to it themselves.

Looking at the athletes who made the finals at the most recent Olympic Games, both men and women were pretty equally divided between the two starts. What's far more important than the type of start used is the speed and distance swimmers obtain when combining the velocity gained from their start with a streamlined entry. Whichever start gives swimmers their best underwater speeds (once they have leveled off from the dive) is the start they should use. So experimentation may be in order.

Drag and the Turn

Second to the start for speed potential is the push-off from the turn. When the word turn is used, I mean not only the motions of changing direction at the wall, but the push-off and any motion (underwater pulls or kicks) prior to the first stroke of the next length. It takes very little effort for swimmers to push off the wall and hold a streamline that will take them five to eight meters down the pool before they take a stroke. Swimmers who do not streamline correctly will be working to get *up* to speed rather than prolonging speed already there. Pushing off the wall in a great streamline is a basic skill for every swimming stroke. Every swimmer should be taught a streamlined push-off and be diligently policed in practicing it. It is amazing to me as I travel to different age-group swim meets how many swimmers push off the wall about two meters (not even past the flags) and take an immediate breath, almost bringing themselves to a stop. What is more amazing is that many coaches let them do this on every turn in every practice without a word being spoken. Proper repetition is important—in practice, in instruction, in everything. Good swimming begins with a good push off the wall. I'll say that again. Good swimming begins with a good push off the wall! A good push off the wall absolutely requires a good streamline, one hand over the other, arms above the head and locked tight over the ears. Swimmers' backs must be straight (not arched), their legs must be together, and most importantly, their feet must be pointed.

Once swimmers have learned streamlined starts, they can combine them with streamlined turns and they will have large portions of their races finished before they take their first strokes. Swimmers who desire to compete at the highest levels must have great turns and the key to great turns is a streamlined push-off. Swimmers who perfect the streamline will greatly benefit their strokes as well, because they will have realized the need for reducing drag. Great swimming begins with a great push-off. There is no substitute.

The streamline position with one hand over the other, shoulders "hyperextended", back flat and feet pointed.

Drag and the Strokes

You may notice that the turn section didn't seem to be about turns at all, but rather about streamlined push-offs. My pointers throughout this book are not so much to detail the "how" as to impress on the reader (hopefully to rub off on the swimmer) the importance in every part of swimming that drag reduction plays. I did not give a detailed account on how to perform a flip turn or a two-hand touch turn. Likewise, I will not completely detail the four strokes, though I do want to cover some *general* aspects of each stroke. Before I do this, I would like to describe the hand position swimmers should use in *all* the strokes. Swimmers should pull with their hands flat, fingertips slightly apart in a relaxed position.

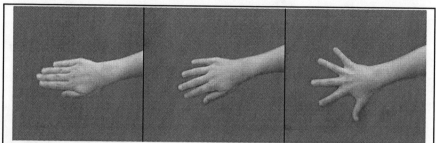

Swimmers should use the hand position seen in the middle picture with their fingers slightly apart.

This hand position creates the largest surface area on the water—more than fingertips together and more than fingertips spread wide. Plus, the forearm muscles don't have to be active to maintain this position. (Less muscle work for finger position means more for swimming fast.)

Something that ties right into streamline is body orientation. Up until the 1990's, coaches taught swimmers to carry their heads fairly high and try to swim *on top of* the water. This body position was especially evident in freestyle and backstroke. However, high head position means lower legs, and instead of swimming through the water flat, swimmers were moving through at an incline. If you think back to the teardrop shape from Chapter 3, this old style of swimming doesn't make sense because low legs in the water mean a large area of drag at the end of the body. Instead, swimmers should be taught to keep their heads and shoulders *down* in the water (by pressing the head and chest down) so that their bodies will be straight and their *feet* will be near the top of the water. This position significantly reduces drag.

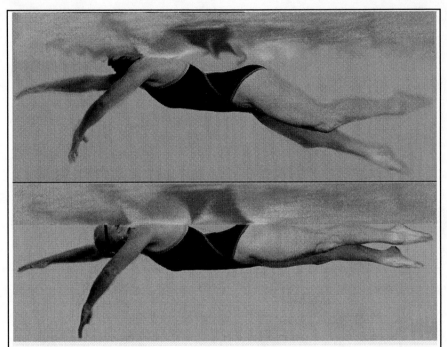

It is easy to see how much more efficient or streamlined the swimmer below is. The position on the bottom can be obtained by forcing the head and shoulders down in the water, which helps the legs stay near the surface.

Freestyle

In freestyle, and actually all the strokes, swimmers can reduce drag by keeping their bodies as long as possible. Australian Olympic Gold Medalist Ian Thorpe provides an excellent example of this when he swims using a modified "catch-up" stroke. A catch-up stroke is when both hands are in front of the head at one point during the stroking pattern. The arm pulling "catches up" to the other in front before that arm makes *its* pull. And *as* that arm makes its pull, the other shoulder joint is "hyperextended" as the swimmer rolls, elongating the body. "Catch-up" also makes a good drill to accentuate the "back" part of the pull, the press past the hips, which is often short-ened or ignored by swimmers.

In the modified catch-up stroke, the left arm is beginning its pull as the right is "hyperextending" forward. This gives the swimmer a stretched, longer body, increasing streamline and decreasing drag.

For swimmers to stay streamlined they should "hyperextend" their forward reaching arms as far forward as possible after they enter the water before starting their pull. This does two things. The most im-portant is that it reduces drag by making the swimmer longer. The second is that it makes each *pull* longer, allowing the swimmer to generate more power with each pull. Interestingly enough, sprinters and not distance swimmers are more likely to swim in the manner de-scribed above. Sprinters need both the reduced drag and the power, whereas too much power in one stroke can fatigue a swimmer pre-maturely in a distance race. Distance swimmers generally prefer to pull more times with less power in each pull (turnover faster).

Regardless of stroke rate and the distance swimmers take *per* stroke, freestylers should pull directly below their bodies. The laws of mechanics (specifically Newton's 3rd Law: For every action, there is an equal and opposite reaction) make this so because any pull more to one side or the other creates a torque which forces the body to move in a direction other than directly down the pool. According to the laws of geometry, the shortest distance between two points is a *straight* line and in this case, the fastest way to get to the other side of the pool is to swim the shortest distance. The better the swimmers, the straighter they swim and visa versa. It is common to see young (10 & under) swimmers zigzagging down the pool. This is partly because they have proportionally large heads compared to their bodies and it can be difficult for them to get their arms around their heads. They eventually *grow* out of *this* difficulty.

The freestyle flutter kick is an important aspect of the freestyle stroke. There are variations, but the two most common kick patterns are the two-beat and the six-beat. The number of beats indicates how many kicks take place during a full arm cycle (right hand entering the water to right hand entering the water again). Two-beat kicks are used largely for balance, with the left foot kicking down as the right arm enters the water and the right foot kicking down as the left arm enters. The two-beat kick is commonly used by distance swimmers because it conserves energy and keeps the body level. Though the six-beat kick uses more energy, it can also generate more propulsion and for this reason it is commonly used by sprinters. As well as during the stroke, kicking should occur off of each wall. Some swimmers will do a few dolphin kicks after freestyle turns and then flutter kick to the surface, while others will just flutter kick. Either way, the flutter kicks must be hard and fast to help the swimmer break the surface at high speed. This is the case whether a swimmer is practicing or competing in sprint or distance. Speed off the wall means faster swimming during the lap with less effort.

Since freestyle is the base stroke for all swimming workouts, every swimmer needs to learn it properly. Freestyle requires a different breathing situation than the other three strokes. From day one, swimmers should learn to breathe every third stroke, meaning they should take three single arm pulls between breaths, breathing on alternate sides. This breathing pattern helps swimmers develop a balanced stroke. It may be that a swimmer will choose a different pattern for *racing*, whether for rhythm or strength or the coach's direction. If so, all *sprinting* practice should be done with *that* pattern (the one used during the meet). Racing can be very difficult for young swimmers if they practice *only* breathing every three and are told at the meet, "Oh, by the way, breathe every five."

So, freestyle is the base stroke for swimming practice. One of the main elements of freestyle is its breathing pattern. Children should practice breathing every three strokes to learn a balanced stroke and develop their muscles symmetrically. Swimmers should stretch their strokes out in front before pulling directly beneath their bodies. Swimmers should kick off every wall and during their stroke. Finally, swimmers should stay level by keeping their shoulders and their heads low in the water.

Backstroke

Today, champion backstrokers in a short course pool can dolphin kick 15 meters underwater, come up, take about three backstroke strokes, spot the flags, take one pull on their sides, take one pull on their stomachs, and flip turn. Backstroke in the way just described does not include many *real* strokes of actual backstroke (strokes on one's back) for a short course race. So, while the stroke of backstroke should be practiced, the other components (the underwater dolphin kick off the wall and the backstroke flip turn) should be practiced just as much or more.

Throughout swimming history, all great backstrokers have had one thing in common—a great kick. Today, fast backstrokers must not only have great backstroke flutter kicks, but also great backstroke *dolphin* kicks. Having a great kick is an advantage for a swimmer in *every* stroke. Children should work on their kicking from the time they first place their feet in the water. In Chapter 3, flexibility of the ankles was discussed as a prerequisite for a great kick. Time spent practicing kicking will help create additional ankle flexibility as well as improve leg strength. Flutter and dolphin kick can be done with a kickboard or without, but underwater kicking is practiced *without* a kickboard.

Just about all children find underwater kicking on their *stomachs* easier than underwater kicking on their backs for two reasons. One reason is that children tend to tuck their chins while performing underwater kicking on their backs. This leads to a non-streamlined, curled up body position and that combination makes their underwater kicking speed slow. For swimmers to become streamlined during underwater kicking on their backs, they must have their heads tucked between their arms and slightly tilted up toward their hands. This will straighten their backs and allow them to kick underwater at maximum speed. Having said that, the reason young swimmers don't *naturally* place their heads in the right position is because it tends to let water up their noses. Since the head really does need to be in this position, here are some ways to adapt. The first one is simply to *let* the water go up the nose and get used to it. This is a difficult one for young swimmers, but many top backstrokers have learned to do it. Another is to curl the upper lip up to plug the nose. Some are genetically inclined to be able do this, others aren't. Still another is to slowly exhale through the nose while on the back. This is probably the most commonly used, but does take a good deal of air that could shorten the underwater streamline—not what you want. One final solution I will present is to use a nose plug. A nose plug should only be a temporary solution, but will help the young swimmer learn the proper underwater position and streamlined push-off without the water-up-the-nose distraction.

When swimmers are actually on top of the water swimming backstroke, the positions of the elbows and hands during the stroke are keys to speed. The hands should enter above and inline with the head, *small finger first*, palm out. As soon as possible, the hand entering the water should turn so that it is pushing water down toward the feet—not out to the sides. To do this, the elbow will bend and both it and the shoulder should be deep in the water, underneath the body for the pull. The hand/wrist/forearm should lead the pull, not the elbow ("dropped elbow"). A good way to work on this stroke outside of the water is by performing the stroke pattern while standing in a doorframe. Small doorframes, like those for a bathroom, force swimmers to rotate. This rotation is required to get the elbow and shoulder beneath (as if it was in the water) the swimmer's body in the best position for a strong pull. A few hundred correctly taken strokes per evening will really reinforce good rotation and proper stroke technique. This same drill can be used in freestyle to help develop rotation and an elbow-higher-than-wrist recovery.

Practicing the backstroke pull in a doorway can enhance your swimmer's ability to pull correctly in the water.

To summarize, all great backstrokers have great flutter and underwater dolphin kicks, and early in a swimmer's career, a lot of time should be spent developing these kicks. As regards the pull, swimmers should concentrate on getting their hands in the position to pull water as soon as possible by getting good body rotation and pulling with their *hands and forearms* as opposed to their elbows during the stroke for more force production.

Butterfly

While butterfly may look difficult for young swimmers to learn, some pick it up quite quickly. The biggest difficulty is actually the breathing. Like great backstrokers, great butterfliers must have great kicks. It is very common today to see swimmers with super dolphin kicks excel in both backstroke and butterfly. This is because, like the rules of backstroke, the rules of butterfly allow swimmers to swim 15 meters of each length underwater. The very good butterfliers can gain a second or more on their competition during every turn. If it's a seven-turn race (like a short course 200), that's seven or more seconds good kickers can distance themselves from their competition. No one can afford to lose that kind of time to another swimmer. Swimmers should *practice* staying underwater and kicking off every turn. This is difficult because swimming butterfly requires *lots* of air. Ankle stretching and practice kicking are important in learning and maintaining a great dolphin kick. There is no other way to gain this.

While a strong kick is essential for butterfly, the arm pull is the most noticeable feature of the stroke. In order to have a proper arm stroke in butterfly with both arms recovering simultaneously over the water, swimmers must have flexible shoulders (see the section on shoulder flexibility). Until swimmers have flexible shoulders, they will struggle with the stroke because they will not be able to get their arms out of the water and/or completely outstretched in front of them.

The key to the butterfly pull is being able to "extend" the arms and "hyperextend" the shoulders at hand entry, then turn the hands and pull directly beneath the body. Also, after breathing, the head should dive down *before* the arms enter the water in front. Otherwise, the head up position sends the legs downward and slows the swimmer. This is a very common fault in young swimmers.

Butterfly, like freestyle, uses a breathing pattern. Though some Olympic Champions breathe every stroke, this is not a good way for a young swimmer to *practice* butterfly. For most swimmers, butterfly requires more energy to take a stroke *with* a breath than to take a stroke *without* a breath. Breathing during butterfly usually creates more drag because raising the face lowers the rest of the body, slowing the swimmer down. For this reason, swimmers should never breathe on their first strokes off the wall, which is when they are trying to maintain that initial speed from their push-offs. When swimmers are young, they can easily learn to breathe every other stroke in butterfly. They should be *required* to do this. As they get older (senior level) they can find the best breathing pattern for them.

To wrap up butterfly, the kick is very important. All butterfliers must have great kicks and should learn to kick underwater off every turn. Butterfliers must have flexible shoulders and must learn to pull directly below their bodies. They should practice breathing every other stroke, putting their faces down before their arms enter, and never breathe on the first stroke off the wall. Turns and finishes require two-hand simultaneous touches.

Breaststroke

Freestyle, butterfly and backstroke all have several things in common. Breaststroke is kind of the odd one out. This is mostly because of flexibility. Breaststroke requires flexible knees and ankles but not in the same direction as the other strokes (some good breaststroke stretches were explained in the section on stretching.). Some swimmers are naturally flexible for breaststroke while others are not, but flexibility is something that swimmers can gain if they work on it. Therefore, there is no reason for swimmers to give up on breaststroke just because they aren't in the group of the "naturally" flexible.

Having described how breaststroke is different from the other three strokes, I should write how it is the same—it requires a streamlined position. At the end of every breaststroke kick, swimmers' arms should be outstretched in front of their heads with faces down, eyes on the bottom of the pool. Their legs should be together, their toes pointed. This is the streamline position for breaststroke, pretty much like the other three strokes. At the end of the kick is when swimmers travel fastest and this streamline position allows them to continue traveling at that highest speed for a short period of time without exerting the effort of another stroke.

The arm pull for breaststroke should be very short and powerful. Swimmers tend to develop their own arm pull lengths and patterns depending on their strengths. A usual breaststroke arm pull is in the shape of a diamond, pulling *only* to a point somewhere under the swimmer's chin or chest. The *hands* can recover (reach forward to the streamline position in front of the swimmer) either above or below the water, but the *elbows* must remain below the water. The hands should only pause once in breaststroke—in the streamline position *after* the kick. It is common for new breaststrokers to pause when they take a breath. This is when their hands are beneath their chins. This is a bad time to stop producing force on the water because it is the least streamlined position during the breaststroke stroke. The last thing about a pull that needs to be said is that when swimmers want to speed up their breaststrokes, the pull *recovery* is the thing they should quicken. In other words, swimmers should throw their hands forward more quickly at the end of each pull when they are trying to sprint.

As is the case for the other strokes, it is difficult to find a great breaststroker without a great kick. The kick used in breaststroke is called the whip kick. In the whip kick, the heels are pulled up close to the buttocks and the toes are turned outward. The knees are closer together than are the feet. The force of the kick is produced from the inside of the foot and to some extent the lower legs, as the feet are "whipped" back. Again, swimmers must have very flexible ankles, feet and knees to get the most out of their kicks. Swimmers who want to be good breaststrokers should work on breaststroke flexibility regularly.

Some breaststrokers will develop knee problems that are associated with the breaststroke kick. It has been found that some of these problems are linked to the *hips* not being flexible enough to rotate (Rovere & Nichols, 1985). Working on hip rotation (see a physical therapist for more information) could help prevent knee injuries in these cases.

One of the most important parts of a breaststroke race is the underwater pull. Good swimmers can take their underwater pulls half-way down a short course pool. This is a must for competitive breast-strokers. I have been to age group meets where one swimmer will take five strokes before another even breaks the surface (ahead). Young swimmers should be required to go a certain distance on every turn. A fun way to do this is to place four coins on the bottom of the pool. A penny is placed at six meters (every swimmer should be able to do this), a nickel at seven meters, a dime at eight meters and a quarter at 10 meters. The game is to see how much money a swimmer can earn (sorry no keeps) on a 100-breaststroke swim. Swimmers add up the value in coins below them as their heads break the surface on their underwater pulls. This makes learning to do the right thing fun.

To wrap up breaststroke, the underwater pull is key to success (even though I put it last). The farther swimmers can go, the better. Arm pulls should start in a diamond pattern, but may change as swimmers develop their strengths. All great breaststrokers have great kicks and flexibility is key to a great kick. And finally, like all the other strokes, fast breaststroke requires a streamline. Like in butterfly, turns and finishes require two-handed simultaneous touches.

A Quick Strokes Wrap-up

Though the four swimming strokes are all different, there are four things I've covered that are important to every one of them. Concentrating on these four things will take a swimmer a long way towards success in swimming. The first is drag reduction. Drag is *the* enemy of all swimmers in all strokes. In every workout, swimmers should seek ways to reduce drag. The most important ingredient to doing this is a great streamline position in which flexible ankles are key. The second thing is time spent underwater. Good swimmers who want to become great swimmers need to work on their underwater streamlines and kicks off every wall at every practice. The third is a powerful pull pattern. All strokes require the high elbow position early in the pull phase of the stroke for maximum power. And the last is a great kick. Strong kicks mean fast swimming and strong kicks come from flexible ankles and lots of time spent kicking.

FIVE

THE WELL-TRAINED SWIMMER

There have been several surges in world record times during the 20th century. One of the biggest was in the 1970's. The 1970's saw the proliferation of training gear items for swimming, including goggles and hand paddles. Until goggles came around, it was difficult to swim for more than a couple of hours a day if you wanted to see during the other 22 hours. Swimming goggles made it possible for swimmers to train more, and they did, up to 20,000 meters in a day! A lot of swimmers from that era are now coaches and coaches tend to train swimmers with what worked for them, hence many train their swimmers with very high mileage.

Here is a question that appeared in *Splash* magazine under, "Ask the experts." "Dear Swim Experts: Lately in practice we have been doing very hard workouts. The other night we did an 8000 IM (that's 2000 straight of each stroke). We have also been practicing for many days a week, including some nights when we practice until about 10:30. It gets very hard to get up and go to school the next day. I just want to know if this is too much for a 12-year-old. I want to get better, but is this the right way? I am beginning to not want to come to practice anymore." This letter could have come from far too many young swimmers around the world and these are not the kinds of thoughts coaches or parents want their swimmers to have. Practices like this *may* improve some young swimmers. However, there is a fine line between distances and workouts that *challenge* and *over-training*. A primary goal of coaches, clubs and parents should be to produce individuals who will continue to enjoy training and competing in the sport of swimming for a long time. The next few sections are guidelines (not absolute rules) to help your swimmer get the most out of the pool and make it to physical maturity as a competitive swimmer.

So, how far should swimmers train in one day? How many *times* a day should swimmers train? How many times a *week* should swimmers train? What do swimmers need to do in workout anyway? These are the questions reviewed in this chapter.

How Far Should Swimmers Train in One Day?

As mentioned, swimmers have been known to swim 20,000 meters a day and perhaps your son or daughter is doing that right now. Marathon runners run around 10-15 miles a day when training for a marathon, a 26.2 mile race. This is about 50% of their race distance. The longest swimming race, the 1500 meters, lasts 15-20 minutes and is only a mile. Long time swimming researcher Dr. David Costill writes that most swimming races are short, no more than 2 minutes and that swimming 3-4 *hours* per day at relatively slow speeds (when compared to race pace) did not help train swimmers for these short maximum efforts (Wilmore & Costill, 1994). Additionally, over-training can cause swimmers to become injured or sick, so caution should be used when ultra-long workouts are chosen.

Are there benefits to swimming 20,000 meters a day? There may be a psychological factor that accompanies swimming "more and harder than other swimmers." If this raises true expectations, then swimmers will swim faster, even if 20,000 meters a day is too much for some of them physically. Another possibility is that swimmers who survive the high workload do so because they become ultra efficient. Somewhere along the many laps in the pool, if swimmers don't quit or get injured, they reduce their drag. Thus, the ones who survive the process have learned how to significantly reduce their drag and I have already detailed how important *that* is. So while researchers have concluded that there may be no cardiovascular or muscular for reason why swimmers to train ultra-distance, that doesn't necessarily mean there can't be some benefit in doing so.

So what is the *best* distance for a swimmer to swim? This completely depends on the swimmer. Since stroke technique is so important for beginner swimmers, no beginners should really do "workouts" until they have the stroke technique to support them. When I say they shouldn't do *workouts*, that means that everything they do should be *practice,* of strokes, turns and starts. Only after they have proper technique should they start to do sets to train their muscles and cardiovascular systems. If they try to train without proper technique, they will end up practicing incorrect form. This has undermined countless swimmers. Again, the adage applies here—"Practice doesn't make perfect. *Perfect* practice makes perfect."

So once swimmers have proper technique, how far should they be swimming a day? That depends on a number of factors, including the swimmer's age, experience, general muscular make-up, and other commitments. Coaches often treat all swimmers the same regardless of the fact that everyone knows no two people are. Now, it is impossible to run a practice for 50 swimmers and give them *all* different workouts, but there should be some consideration to break a large group of swimmers into smaller groups and it is likely that your swimmer's coach already does this.

One might think that means the IMers will swim with the IMers, the distance swimmers with distance swimmers and sprinters with sprinters. This is probably not a good way to do things. Some senior level distance swimmers don't need to swim far—5,000 meters a day is tops for them. Some senior level sprinters may need 8,000 meters a day. In general, most IMers need more meters of just stroke work because they have four strokes to perfect. So I can't answer the question of how many meters a day a swimmer should train because it varies with the physical make-up of each swimmer and not just what strokes the swimmer competes in.

There have been swimmers who perform superbly on 3,000 a day (everything is hard) and there is some scientific basis for why this might work. Most need more. The following are some guidelines for daily workout distances for different age-groups.

Some general guidelines for daily swimming

8 & U   1000-2500 meters/yards per day
9 & 10   1500-3000 meters/yards per day
11 & 12   3000-6000 meters/yards per day
13 & 14   4000-8000 meters/yards per day
15 & Up   5000-12,000 meters/yards per day

How Many Times a Day Should a Swimmer Train?

Studies have shown that swimmers who swim twice a day do not show improvements over those who train once a day (Costill et al., 1991, Mostardi et al., 1975, Watt et al., 1973). They don't need the cardiovascular work of two workouts a day. Swimmers *may* benefit from two workouts a day, however, if one practice is solely devoted to skill work, providing the extra workout doesn't cause something else critical to performance to suffer—sleep, nutrition, mental well-being or schoolwork. Now, if the swimmer has nothing to do all day other than swim (on the national team or during a break from school, for instance) two-a-days might be okay. Usually though, young swimmers must go to school during the day, have homework to do and some socializing too. Two workouts a day can place a huge burden on these swimmers.

The decision to do two-a-day workouts, like so many things in swimming, should be based on the individual swimmer. It can be difficult for coaches, swimmers and, yes, you parents to get beyond the concept that if one workout is good, two should be better. There *are* some swimmers out there who *do* benefit from two workouts a day. Some receive no *benefit* from two workouts a day, but the extra session also causes no *harm*. Others are physically or psychologically debilitated by multiple workouts. Treating all swimmers the same will ruin some swimmers and mentally burn out some others. Parents should keep a close eye on their swimmers who are swimming very hard, whether in two workouts a day or one very long workout. Swimmers who do not sleep well at night, are losing their appetites or are losing interest in doing well in other activities (school) should be brought to the coach's attention. More is *not* better and swimming is not everything in life. Kids need a chance to be kids.

It should always be the swimmer's and/or parent's decision to swim more than once a day, never solely the swim club's decision. Look at it from the parent's side. If parents have to devote considerable time to transporting a child to and from swim practices both in the mornings and in the evenings, family time will be compromised. In most homes, at least one parent works, and in many homes, both parents work. If a child is at swim practice during the hours the parents are *not* working, there is little time for child-parent or family interaction. This period of time in a child's life only comes around once and it should not be missed. In addition, parents know their children well enough to know if they need, want and are physically durable enough to swim twice a day. As the financial backers of age-group programs, you as parents have a responsibility to help provide guidelines.

Should a swimmer swim twice a day?

12 & U	No
13 & 14	Under special circumstances (agreement of swimmer, coach and parent)
15 & Up	Depends on the swimmer

How Many Times a Week Should a Swimmer Train?

This not only depends on the swimmer, but the time of year (whether during school or break). First I will discuss the school week. So with that in mind, let's start with the young swimmers. Notice that I'm not classifying children into skill levels, but by age. An eight and under swimmer, David, who swims every day, may become an eight and under champion and possibly a 9-10 champion, but very likely won't realize his *full* potential, because by the time his body and mind become strong enough to really swim fast (15 or older), he will have had enough swimming and want nothing to do with a pool. I believe children under the age of 9 should probably not practice more than twice a week during the school year (possibly three times if they are just learning the swimming skills or getting ready for a big meet). In the summer, they can practice more because there is still plenty of a playtime during the day. The most important things for young swimmers are that they learn the skills correctly and *enjoy* swimming.

I've already discussed how difficult swimming is to learn. Some children may get in the water and not like it and dread going to swim practices. Don't let this stop you from taking them. Kids often don't like things they have to struggle at, and they *will* struggle at first learning to swim. Once they make some friends, go to a few meets and see some improvements, though, their attitudes will likely change. If you have to drag your child to practice every day and you've been doing it for over a year, however, you may want to rethink things. There could be some good reasons to continue, like for controlling asthma or weight, but barring these reasons, it may be time to change activities for your child.

For the 9-10 age group, I would say a good rule of thumb is 3 practices per week during the school year. For the 11-12 age group, I would say 4 per week. Once children turn 13 and love to swim, turn them loose. One thing to note here is that if the swimmer is competing during the weekends, either on one day or both, then they are actually swimming more than the set number of days I have described above. That is okay. An 11-year-old may then swim 6 days a week if they compete on both Saturday and Sunday. Swim meet days should not be considered practice days.

Up to now, I have been writing about swimming year round. This is probably a good place to talk about whether swimming year round is a good thing. Some of the goals parents should have for their swimmers are; to become technically correct at all the strokes, to perform starts and turns with excellent technique/streamline, and to learn good racing strategies. Once children can do these things, *then* they can take time off swimming and come back to the sport bigger, stronger, and faster after a break. The skills they have learned will come back to them quickly. Now, no swimming coach wants a swimmer who *has* these skills to stop swimming, but if the swimmer is tired of it or wants to pursue another activity for a season, this may not be the end of a swimming career. On the other hand, swimmers who stop swimming *without* these skills/techniques will have a difficult time catching up to the other swimmers in their age groups if they want to start again. This might lead to a discouraged swimmer who could end up quitting for good. Swimming is a lifelong skill. It is worth having kids learn it and learn it correctly. So what I'm saying is, don't let your child(ren) stop swimming until they have become technically correct at all the strokes, can perform starts and turns with excellent technique/streamline, and have learned good racing strategies. This is kind of a ploy, since once they have learned these things, they will be pretty competitive and they won't likely *want* to stop swimming.

Speaking of summer training, I have so far referred to the *school* year in regards to how many times a week children should swim. What about during the summer? During the summer, or breaks (like Christmas), children can swim every day no matter what their age. If your child seems overly tired, then you might want to change the weekly practice number, but otherwise break times are good opportunities to do some concentrated swimming without the added stress of school.

One last note on number of practices per week; hopefully, your club doesn't offer only two sessions a week to 8 and under swimmers, three to 9-10s and so on. If a team offers practice times only twice a week and the 8 and under swimmer misses one, then that swimmer is not in fact practicing twice a week. The best situation is when a swim club offers numerous practices per week and families have the option of selecting practice times based on the demands of a specific week.

What Should Swimmers do in Workout Anyway?

To this point I have been trying not to use the words *workout* and *practice* interchangeably. I define "practice" as practicing a skill. Practice is very important in the sport of swimming, as I have said already. The question was, however, "What should swimmers do in *workout* anyway?" The word "workout" means to physically train.

Though this section is about the *physical* adaptations that occur from workout, the most important adaptations that occur from workout are *mental*. Swimmers learn how to endure fatigue. They learn coping strategies of how to deal with the pain they force on themselves. They learn how to do it for longer and longer periods of time. They learn how to concentrate on a skill, though they are tired. These are things that swimmers learn in workout that they can apply at meets.

In addition to these very important mental changes, workouts change the body physically. This section will detail changes to the blood, the heart and the muscles.

The bloodstream carries oxygen and nutrients to the muscles. When muscles work, the increased need for oxygen triggers the human body to produce more red blood cells *and* more blood. More red blood cells carry more oxygen to the working muscles and the increase in plasma (the watery portion of the blood) keeps the blood from becoming too thick (which is very bad). So, workouts increase blood volume and red blood cells.

Workouts make the heart work harder. The heart as a muscle gets larger and stronger if stressed. A larger and stronger heart means more blood is pumped with each beat, taking more blood and hence more oxygen to muscles.

There are two general types of muscle fibers within skeletal muscles (movement muscles), slow twitch and fast twitch. Slow twitch muscle fibers are associated with endurance efforts while fast twitch muscle fibers are associated with sprints. Each of these muscle fiber types can be specifically trained to improve endurance or sprint capacity respectively. Most workouts are designed to stress muscles aerobically, meaning "with air", which works on endurance/slow twitch fibers. One of the most significant ways muscles adapt to *aerobic* work is by increasing the number of mitochondria (the powerhouses of cells), which allows them to produce more energy with the help of oxygen. This adaptation makes training for distance events meaningful.

Fast twitch muscle fibers are *anaerobic,* "without oxygen" fibers and do not require oxygen to contract. Without air, muscles get around 18 times less energy than they do *with* air from the same molecule of fuel. Also, they produce a substance known as lactic acid, the build-up of which is believed to cause muscle failure or fatigue. Fast twitch fibers *are*, however, big and can produce a *lot* of force, much more than slow twitch fibers. At a highly competitive level, swimming events 200 meters and below (that's most swimming events!) use significantly more *fast* than slow twitch fibers.

So, on to training. It seems obvious that since most swimming events use predominately fast twitch muscles, workouts should be written to exercise predominantly fast twitch (*an*aerobic) muscles. Maybe so, but most workouts are written more aerobic. It hurts quite a bit more to work anaerobically than aerobically and anaerobic work requires more rest between swims, which makes for inefficient use of limited pool time. Hey, we all have to get our money's worth, right? I guess what I'm saying is that, physiologically speaking, swimmers need more anaerobic work than most programs provide. That is not to say that swimmers should get in the pool, swim a bunch of fast swims and then take a shower. Aerobic work is good not only for providing better cardiovascular fitness, but it also allows time for stroke and drag reduction technique work. A *combination* of aerobic and anaerobic work in each workout is good.

You may have noticed that swimmers don't train the same as long distance runners. There is seldom a day where you hear a coach say, let's go for an hour and a half straight and get out. Swimmers swim *intervals* and it's a good thing, because the view of the line on the bottom of the pool gets very old on long swims. A typical interval set might be 20 X 100 free on 1:30. This means every minute and thirty seconds, swimmers start a 100 freestyle, and they do this 20 times. Swimmers may do this set in many different ways. They may work a specific drill on numbers 5-10, they may try to go faster each one (*descend*), they may intermix a stroke or kick, or they may just swim them, racing each one against swimmers in the next lane. By doing any of these things, and there are hundreds of ways to swim a set of one-hundreds, swimmers have something else to concentrate on other than the line on the bottom of the pool.

The above was an example of an *aerobic* set. Here is a change to make it an *anaerobic* set. 6 X 100 on 6:00 from the starting blocks, looking for best average. This set allows swimmers enough rest to work very hard on each 100. Every swim, swimmers will collect lactic acid and some lactic acid will be worked off during the rest period while the remainder is present for the next 100. By the last 100, it really hurts. In this kind of set, swimmers get a chance to swim fast and race one another, something many find very motivating.

Training Wrap Up

This chapter was written to help *keep* swimmers swimming. It's very easy for parents and coaches to look at talented 9 or 11-year olds and think, if we work them out six days a week, sometimes twice a day, having them swim 8000 meters a day for the next year (they'll still be in the same age group), then they'll have a chance to set some

THE PARENTS' GUIDE TO SWIMMING

national records. The training guidelines discussed in this chapter may not provide a lot of 10 and 12-year old National Champions, but they *should* provide a lot more motivated 15 – 22-year old *swimmers* down the line. The topic of keeping swimmers swimming and competing will be further covered in Chapter 9, Swimming Burnout.

SIX

SWIMMING NUTRITION

In the previous chapters, I have attempted to educate parents on ways to help their children become better swimmers, both psychologically and physically. Some things were written as suggestions for instruction, others simply to educate the parent on good swimming. When it comes to nutrition, the proverb, "You are what you eat." is appropriate. In this chapter, I will cover nutritional requirements for swimmers, carbo-loading and what to eat the days before a meet, and what swimmers should eat the day of and during a meet. I am going to assume that the reader has *some* knowledge of nutrition, but if anything in this chapter is strange (like what is a carbohydrate), I suggest the reader pick up a book on nutrition before continuing.

Nutritional Requirements for Swimmers

Humans need to consume carbohydrates, fats, proteins, minerals, vitamins and water. There are several different philosophies with respect to the percentages of the three different fuels active individuals need to eat, but the U.S. Department of Agriculture (USDA) says that humans should consume 60% carbohydrates, 30% fats and 10% proteins. Most experts believe that athletes do not need different proportions than non-athletes, they just need more *calories* overall. The FDA nutritional labels required on foods in the U.S. make this task simpler, but it can be difficult to balance each *meal* to the 60/30/10 percentages. It is often easier to balance out a *day*.

The percentages of carbohydrates, fats and proteins are for the *average* person and you may have noticed that I don't define anyone as average. You may wish to tweak your child's diet and observe the resulting performance, but don't do this the week before an important meet. Some swimmers need more carbohydrates; others seem to do well on lots of fat. It is important to know your child because a swimmer who feels good in practice swims faster, and swimming faster practices changes swimmers' true expectations of their racing, producing faster racing.

Some good sources of carbohydrates are grains, including breads, cereals, rice and pasta. Simple sugars are also carbohydrates, table sugar and chocolate are examples, but these carbohydrates do not contain as many complex polymers as other carbohydrate sources (like potatoes) and thus do not provide the body with as much energy. A traditional breakfast favorite for swimmers is pancakes because they are high in complex carbohydrates. Most nutritionists would recommend staying away from the simple sugars—"simple sugars for simple minds"—but they *can* be "feel good foods" and feeling good can raise true expectations . . . you get the idea.

Fats are found in almost everything it seems, and food labels highlight fats, putting them near the top of the list. Because of this, fats in food products seem to have become the enemy. But swimmers need fat. In fact, that's what they burn for energy most of the day, and unless you are pedaling furiously on a stationary bike while you're reading this, *you* are burning mostly fat right now too. Fat is *not* the enemy. It is an essential part of a well balanced diet. Don't *over*do, of course, but don't take fat *from* your child's diet either. Fat is found in dairy products, meats, snacks and many other foods that we like to eat.

Protein is an incredible and necessary substance for our bodies. Proteins support our body's cells and tissues. Our muscles are *made* of proteins (actin and myosin). We have proteins called enzymes that help speed up chemical reactions in our bodies. And we have hormones that are protein-*based*, such as insulin, which is essential for transporting blood sugar. Within each red blood cell lie 250,000 protein molecules called hemoglobin that transport oxygen to our body tissues. In addition to all these other duties, protein can be broken down and used as a source of energy, though it is not our bodies' first choice.

Proteins are comprised and broken down by digestion into 20 different amino acids. Some are essential, that we must *consume*, while others are non-essential and our bodies make them for us. Most balanced diets provide enough of the essential amino acids. Fad diets can lack certain essential amino acids, and suffice it to say it's not good to be short on amino acids because a deficit of one or another could prevent the body from forming a specific protein needed to sustain life.

Many people ask about taking extra protein. It stands to reason that since muscles are made of protein and humans need protein to build and strengthen muscles, athletes would need more than non-athletes. To this end, tremendous amounts of money are spent each year on protein supplements. Personally, I do not recommend them. Since athletes are eating more food, they are also eating more protein. There should be enough protein in a balanced diet that protein supplementation is not necessary.

When excess protein is broken down and used as fuel for the body, it contains a nitrogen group that once broken off from the rest of the protein molecule, becomes ammonia. Ammonia is toxic to the body and the body converts it into urea. Urine high in urea has a very strong odor (like cat urine). Basically, excess protein makes for very expensive and stinky urine.

Vitamin supplements can *also* make the urine expensive. A balanced diet should provide enough vitamins for healthy living. Athletes actually *do* need more of some vitamins than non-athletes, but again, athletes *eat* more than non-athletes, taking in more vitamins along with the calories. Does this mean I'm not endorsing the taking of vitamins? No. It is very difficult to take in a perfectly balanced diet. Probably very few people do. If that pertains to your child, then taking vitamins on a regular basis is not a bad idea. However, a regular basis may be every other day or twice a week. Here are some things about vitamins you may not know that could affect your swimmer.

There are two categories of vitamins, water-soluble and fat-soluble. Water-soluble vitamins include vitamin C and the B complex vitamins (often listed by their individual names, like Riboflavin which is B2). The fat-soluble vitamins are A, D, E and K. Individuals who take too much of the water-soluble vitamins during a day will find that their bodies will process the excess vitamins and get rid of them in the urine—it will be bright yellow (this deep color can also be caused by dehydration, however.). This is not a harmful thing for the body if the overdose of these vitamins is not grossly excessive. Fat-soluble vitamins are a bit different. Excess amounts of *fat*-soluble vitamins are not expelled from the body, but are absorbed in the body's fat ("fat-soluble"). Once in the fat, the excess vitamins become toxic to the body. Now, here is the real problem for swimmers, especially male swimmers. Some swimmers have very low amounts of body fat, and if there is not much body fat to absorb the excess fat-soluble vitamins, then there is a high toxic buildup in the small amount of fat that is there. It is simple math with respect to toxicity. This is why I do not recommend taking vitamins on a *daily* basis.

Minerals are not quite the same as vitamins. Our bodies must have several different minerals in order to function properly. To fire one muscle cell, our body uses potassium, sodium and calcium. An integral part of our oxygen carrying capability is iron, which is in every molecule of hemoglobin in our blood. Athletes and non-athletes alike around the world could be suffering from a lack of proper mineral balance; because farmlands have lost the minerals they once had and therefore, so have our foods. In the next decade or two, mineral supplementation may overtake vitamin supplementation. While working out, swimmers tend to sweat out a lot of minerals. Because of their high exercise loads, they will need more minerals than an average child their age. One of the ways to provide these is to purchase *liquid* minerals, which can be poured into a breakfast drink. Extra minerals might not be a bad idea for the entire family.

Water is probably the most important and overlooked substance that a swimmer intakes daily. Even a little dehydration can impede performance. It is often thought that because swimmers are in cool water, they don't sweat. This is not true. Unfortunately, because they are in water, swimmers don't often think about the fact that they are sweating and losing water, and therefore don't drink. Twenty years ago, swimmers never drank during workouts. Today, thankfully, many coaches demand that swimmers have water bottles on deck and that they stay hydrated.

A question that is always asked, "Is it better to drink water or a sports drink?" Water is cheaper and may be better for your swimmer, but swimmers (and others) may like the taste of sports drinks and therefore drink more of them than they would water. If a swimmer will drink water, water is what that swimmer should drink. If not, dilute a sports drink with water.

I have avoided to this point telling any personal stories, but here is one I think should go in this book. I was at the U.S. Olympic Training Center in Colorado in an elite camp. We had about 20 athletes there and an exercise scientist did a complete blood work-up on all of us. Every one of the 20 athletes in the group was low on stored iron, (17 on the low range of normal). There were three that were well below the normal range and they were all vegetarians. One woman, whose performance had been visibly dropping off for the previous few months had about 1/4 of the stored iron that would have placed her on the bottom of normal range. The staff at the Olympic Training Center was so alarmed at our group they sent a nutrition Ph.D. in to speak with us. This man stood in front of us and actually slammed his fist on the table and said, "You must eat red meat." He didn't say you must eat chicken or fish, he said "red meat." There is a reason for this. Red meat contains essential nutrients that our bodies can easily process, iron being one of them and essential amino acids are others. Swimmers need these! Now, if your swimmer doesn't eat red meat for religious reasons, I'm not here to say give up your beliefs. Beliefs are more important than the sport of swimming. However, if you don't have your swimmer eating red meat because you think it is unhealthy, rethink this and talk to a sports nutritionist.

Carbo-loading

When the human body is working at peak intensity (like during most swimming races and practices), it wants to burn carbohydrates. Because of this, most swimmers should consume meals rich in carbo-hydrates, especially on the days leading up to a swimming meet. This is one kind of "carbo-loading". But before continuing with the differ-ent ways to carbo-load, I'll give a short background on energy sys-tems.

The body can use carbohydrates, fats and proteins to produce en-ergy. When the body is resting and when it is working at low inten-sity, it uses 100% fat for fuel. Most humans, even the skinny ones, have *weeks* of fuel stored as fat. As the intensity of an activity in-creases (this can be measured by heart rate), the body starts to burn some carbohydrates, so there is a mixture of fat and carbohydrate use. Once the intensity of physical work reaches a high level, the body can only burn carbohydrates. All swimming races are intense enough that the body should only be burning carbohydrates. If the body runs out of carbohydrates to burn, it will not be able to work at the same in-tense level. This is often referred to as "hitting the wall". Humans have about a two-hour potential storage capacity for carbohydrates.

Since no swimming pool event lasts for two or more hours, you might figure that swimmers get plenty of carbohydrates in their nor-mal diets and don't need to load up on them. This is probably a mis-take, especially in age group swimming where it is common for swimmers to be competing off and on for several hours plus warm-up. Swimmers will burn quite a lot of carbohydrates during warm-up. They will also burn carbohydrates in *anticipation* of a race, *during* a race and *after* the race. If their races are equally spread out, they will burn carbohydrates for several hours (though not at the level they would if they were swimming very hard the entire time). Still, this may be enough for them to hit the wall or "bonk" on their last race. So, having an abundance of carbohydrates in the body is a good thing.

To do this, swimmers can *carbo-load*. There have been several different methods tested for carbo-loading. One is to starve the body of carbohydrates about a week out from a big swim meet, and then two days in advance, pack in the carbohydrates. This method tends to trick the body into storing *more* carbohydrates than it normally would. I don't recommend this method of carbo-loading because for the week leading up to the big meet, when swimmers are eating no carbohydrates, they tend to feel terrible. Feeling terrible can lower their true expectations of their upcoming performances, which is the worst thing that can happen. Instead, most swimmers should just change their diets a couple of days away from a big meet to include a greater percentage of carbohydrates. This form of carbohydrate loading is really pretty easy to implement. Oh, and by the way, carbohydrates need water to store, so swimmers should drink plenty of liquid those few days before the meet too. This can also help with any latent dehydration problems.

Now that I have explained a good deal about carbohydrates, I will relate why it is important that swimmers get enough during their normal, non-competition days. Swimming workouts can tap swimmers of carbohydrates pretty quickly. If this happens, they won't swim as fast in practice, which will lead to a possible detrimental change in true expectations and hence in future performances. So make sure your kids get a snack after school to fuel up before afternoon or evening practice. One more thing here—the body tends to do a very good job storing carbohydrates immediately following an intense workout when carbohydrate stores have been depleted. Food intake (mostly carbohydrates) should occur within two hours of finishing a workout (Burke, 2000). In most cases, sooner is better. So, fairly quickly following a workout, swimmers should have a meal or snack high in carbohydrates to best replenish their carbohydrate stores.

Swimming Meet Nutrition

If a swim meet is during the afternoon, some four or more hours after breakfast, then a big breakfast of carbohydrates is probably a good thing. If the meet is in the morning, and many age group meets are, then large amounts of carbohydrates are to be avoided during the hour or so prior to the meet (this includes warm-up too). It is probably best to have a light meal with a pretty high fat content. This is because the body tends to go into a low blood sugar period after eating a high carbohydrate meal. Low blood sugar periods can leave athletes with a lethargic feeling, which can lower their true expectations of their performances and a sub-par performance may be the result. I hope by this point you understand how pretty much everything plays into your swimmer's true expectations?

The most important thing for swimmers to consume during a meet is water. This is especially true when the meet is outdoors and it is hot. Swimmers who are thirsty already have their performances impaired. Swimmers get nervous before races, so they sweat and they need to go to the bathroom a lot. If they drink, they should be seeing clear urine during all those trips. The three best things for swimmers to consume during a swim meet are water, water and water. Again, if a swimmer doesn't like the taste of water and would drink a sports drink more readily, mix water with a sports drink to keep your swimmer hydrated.

Depending on the length of the meet, swimmers don't have to eat anything during it. However, if a meet is long, four hours or over, then some food is good. The best thing for swimmers to do is eat small amounts of food throughout the meet. It may be a good idea to train swimmers to swim with something in their stomachs, so that when they get older and more competitive, they won't have trouble eating prior to and during meets.

There are several packaged products that can be consumed at meets, but many are on the dry side and are kind of heavy feeling in the stomach. They are not usually the first choice of swimmers. There are also packaged gels, which are a pretty good idea since they go down easy. They *are* expensive. One of the easiest and best things for swimmers to eat is a mix consisting of small crackers, nuts, cereal, pretzels and dried fruits. Some candy bits can be mixed in to add flavor. Know what your swimmer likes. Another good snack is fruit. Bananas have always been a good swimming food along with peaches and grapes—the last two have the advantage of having high water content. Here is a short warning about *too* much fruit, however. A high fruit diet *can* cause diarrhea, so be conservative if you don't know your child's reaction to fruit.

Swimming Nutrition in a Nutshell

There will always be questions about what is good nutrition. The USDA food pyramid is under attack and in truth probably has some flaws to it. Two researchers have come out with a new pyramid that seems to correct some of the flaws (Willett & Stampfer, 2003). But their pyramid is not specifically designed for athletes, swimmers, or your swimmer in particular. It is hard to know whether what you read about nutrition is correct since it seems to change every year. Because of this, take what I have written as a guideline. From there, you will need to find what works best for your swimmer.

SEVEN

SWIMMING EQUIPMENT

Today's swimmer arrives at the pool carrying a stuffed mesh bag. What are all those things inside? At first introduction to swimming, parents might think that it's a relatively inexpensive sport. What is there to buy, a suit and some goggles?—That has to be better than a horse and a saddle. Well, there is a bit more to it than that. That swim bag is filled with fins, paddles, a pull-buoy, a kickboard and possibly a piece of old bicycle tubing. What are all these items for? Read on.

Swimming Suits

The swimsuit is the most important piece of swimming equipment. I say this since I have yet to see someone race without one (though I have seen a few slip down). There are several different styles of swimming suits and costs vary with the style. Most suits are made of a Lycra blend. Lycra makes suits stretch, which makes them comfortable. It also makes suits fit tightly enough that they reduce drag while the athlete is swimming. Lycra suits do tend to stretch and wear out fairly quickly, though today's suits are getting better. Durability-wise, nylon is a good material and hence makes a good practice suit, though nylon suits tend to be a bit baggy, so they are not generally used for racing.

Because suits wear out, swimmers should have separate suits for practice and racing. Swimmers shouldn't wear their racing suits to practice or they will become stretched out and begin to create excess drag. Swim teams will change their team suits every so often and when they do, the old team suit can become a practice suit.

As you may have observed when shopping for a suit, swim suits are pricey. Traditional girl's/women's suits can cost twice as much as traditional men's suits and I haven't even talked about the new Fastskin suits. Be frugal and buy practice suits that are on sale or discontinued. Also, most manufactures offer "Grab bag" suits that can be good deals.

You may have noticed older swimmers wearing two or more suits at practice. Sometimes pieces of these swimmers' suits are torn and are dangling down their legs. Swim practice is not a fashion show, but it should not be a grunge contest either. Some boys will wear a pair of beach shorts to practice. They may be doing this because they like the look of them. Or they might think they are training with a greater drag which will make them stronger. I don't suggest wearing beach-type shorts on a full-time basis because they do significantly increase drag and that can change the way your swimmer swims, both the body position and the speed. Swimmers need to swim fast in practice to be ready to swim fast in meets. If a coach wants the swimmers to wear drag-type suits, the coach will let them know on which sets they should be worn.

It is important to rinse suits out in the shower at the end of every practice. This gets some of the pool chemicals out of the suit. Swimsuits should be unwadded and put out to dry each evening. Don't leave suits rolled up in a towel for the next practice or they will be wet the next practice time (or frozen if left overnight in a car during a northern winter). Cold wet suits are not fun to put on the next day. If a wet suit is left in a towel overnight in the south, it is going to mildew. This can cause skin problems as well as make the suit wear out faster.

Some parents may ask, "When do I buy my swimmer a Fastskin suit?" Others may ask, "What *is* a Fastskin suit?" Fastskin suits are the body or partial body suits that first came to the public's attention during the 2000 Sydney Olympics. The material used to make these suits creates very little drag in the water—really not different than shaved skin. What these suits may do is: 1) change swimmers true expectations—swimmers think the *suit* is faster and therefore so are they, 2) trap air between the skin and the suit and therefore add buoyancy that in the long run creates less drag, and/or 3) compress the muscles, which helps blood return to the heart and improves circulation. Any of these could help a swimmer go faster either physically or psychologically.

When should a swimmer get one? Swimmers who believe that they can't compete without one (which is a shame) might consider it. Fastskins are very expensive (and might make you think about switching your child's sport to equestrian after all). Truly, though, I would not recommend getting a Fastskin suit until your swimmer is competing at a regional (state, province, etc.) championship (high school age), zone championship (age 15 and older) or national level. If they swim in college, then the college will buy the suit. By the way, these suits tend to adsorb water after which they loose their benefits. So, if your swimmer has one, it should only be warn to race and it should be dried off between races.

Goggles

Buying a pair of goggles is not as simple as it might seem. There are many different kinds of goggles on the market. The differences include size and shape, lens color, fog-free or anti-fog coatings, nosepieces, and the type of cushioning they use or don't use against the eyes.

Having uncomfortable goggles during practice can make practice miserable and having goggles that fit well and stay on during a race is imperative for good swims. Just as with suits, swimmers should have more than one pair of goggles. Generally, swimmers can find productive use for as many as four different pairs. Swimmers should not use the same pair of goggles for practice that they do in a meet. There are a number of reasons for this. The first is because goggles wear out and loose their seal and swimmers are more likely to feel the effects of this when they dive off the block at a meet. Also, swimmers should wear their meet goggles tighter than their practice goggles. Young and old swimmers alike are prone to forget to tighten their goggles before their first race and this can lead to goggles in the mouth or around the neck shortly after the dive. Another reason is the shading factor. Swimmers who practice or swim meets outside (especially if they swim backstroke) will want goggles that provide some UV protection. Check the goggle package to make sure it says it provides UV protection. (Don't assume because it is darker in color that it provides UV protection.)

Before anti-fog coatings came to be, the first thing swimmers did when they got to the pool was to lick or spit into their goggles. Spit provided some natural anti-fogging. Anti-fog goggles have put an end to spit for many. I highly recommend them.

Regarding cushioning against the eyes, Swedish goggles don't have any. Many top-notch swimmers wear Swedish goggles. This doesn't mean they are better than other kinds of goggles. But a warning to those parents whose children switch to Swedish goggles. Because these goggles don't have cushioning gaskets, they can leave sore spots around the eyes for the first week or so.

Some goggles have gaskets that are hypoallergenic, which prevent eye or skin irritation from goggles for many swimmers. Silicone gaskets and the no gasket Swedish goggles are hypoallergenic. Some goggles have foam gaskets and are not hypoallergenic. I do not recommend foam personally, though many people find them perfectly acceptable.

A good bet for young swimmers is a silicone-plastic gasket goggle with anti-fog lenses. If the child swims outside, look for one tinted "smoke" with UV protection. If the child swims inside, clear or yellow are good choices.

Here is one last thing about goggles for swimmers without 20/20 vision. There *are* prescription goggles. This doesn't help swimmers see underwater as much as it helps them see the pace clock, the coach's face, etc. If your child's vision is worse than 20/200, you might want to look into prescription goggles. If your child wears contact lenses, they can usually wear them *under* normal goggles. If they race in the lenses, it is wise to have them wear the disposable kind. Otherwise goggles coming off during a start could be costly for both swimmer *and* parent.

Caps

Both boys and girls can wear swim caps. Generally, boys with relatively short hair will not wear caps during practice. Girls almost always wear caps during practice regardless of hair length. A swimming cap can keep the hair collected and reduce drag. Even the longest hair can somehow be tucked under a swimming cap. Swimming caps also help save on pool maintenance. Long hair is the enemy of most pool filters.

Swim caps are usually made of latex or silicone but also come in Lycra. Lycra caps are probably the most comfortable, but like suits tend to stretch. Latex or silicone caps maintain their shapes better, though they can tear and when they do, they have to be tossed. This will happen a couple of times a year for swimmers who wear one every day.

Swim caps are actually made to reduce drag (not just hold the hair in) and that's why swimmers wear them during races. Another way of reducing hair drag is to shave. There may be little physical difference between a shaved head and a swimming cap (in other words, the drag they produce is similar), but some swimmers receive a psychological boost from the feeling of a shaved head.

Caps are the most visible part of a swimmer attire during a race. Because of this, most teams print their logos on their caps. Of course, from a parent's perspective, the most important thing about a swimming cap is that it helps the parent spot swimmers on their child's team. A team that is savvy about identifying their swimmers will pick a cap color unlike any other team's.

Kickboards

A kickboard is a floatation device that aids swimmers when kicking. The traditional kickboard is tombstone shaped and made from a rugged Styrofoam. There are several shapes and styles of kickboards on the market today. Some can be used as kickboards *and* pull-buoys. Some are soft and flexible.

In general the best kickboards are the traditional tombstone shaped boards. I personally like the stiffer ones because they provide more support and can last for twenty plus years. One thing to look for in a kickboard is that it doesn't over-float your swimmer. Swimmers who weigh less than 100 pounds (45 kg) should get a Jr. kickboard that is a bit smaller. They should stay with the smaller kickboard as long as it works for them. Kickboards that float too much can make kicking practice less effective by placing swimmers in an unnatural kicking position. Kickboards that don't float *enough* can make it difficult for swimmers to breathe while kicking, so middle ground is good.

Fins

Fins and swim fins are not necessarily the same thing. Swimmers wear fins because: 1) they help ankle flexibility, 2) they add stress to the swimming kick, 3) they help develop good kicking technique, and 4) they make swimmers feel fast. The extra force placed on the edge of fins helps extend a swimmer's ankles, which in turn helps to create a more flexible ankle. This reason alone is why many coaches have their swimmers use fins. Fins also help place more stress on the leg muscles and this is the equivalent of adding weights to the kick. Fins can help young swimmers get the rhythm and technique of the more difficult dolphin kick. Fins can also provide the feel of fast swimming without the actual tiring effort, letting kids practice the feel of this faster pace.

The best swim fins for flutter and dolphin kick are usually only a few inches longer than swimmers' feet. They should also be twice as wide as the foot. This will give swimmers the power and stretch that fins are designed to create without feeling too different from the swimmers' actual feet. (You don't want to get long SCUBA fins.) Training fins have a variety of prices and in this case, the more expensive ones are usually the ones to buy. Since fins last a long time, you might consider a trade-up/down system on your team.

Another type of fin is for the breaststroke whip kick. These fins are called "positive drive" fins and seem to help breaststrokers get more power out of their kicks. It is unclear if these fins will cause any long-term knee damage, as they *do* place a lot of pressure on the knee joint. Currently, I would not recommend children under 13-years old wear these fins. The coach will ultimately be the decision maker for the positive drive fins because if they are not incorporated in a workout, your child doesn't need them. By the way, I *do* recommend *regular* swimming fins even for beginner swimmers because swimming fins can be an effective teaching tool for both kick and stroke technique.

There is one last thing about fins. They can be worn over a pair of socks to avoid possible heal blisters; so you might want to add a pair of socks to that swim bag.

Paddles

Paddles give swimmers a larger hand surface area, which creates more resistance on the water during an arm pull. This resistance can basically be thought of as arm weights for swimming.

Paddles are made of plastic and come in many shapes and sizes. In general, swimmers should get hand-shaped paddles that are slightly bigger than their hands. Paddles with holes in them let the water flow more evenly and keep the paddle stable during pulling. There are paddles specifically designed to correct stroke flaws and a parent might want to ask the coach if this might help.

Most swimmers and coaches think that paddles are for older swimmers, but I especially like paddles for beginner swimmers to improve stroke technique. Paddles can help correct improper hand position if a swimmer tends to swim with curled hands or fists. Paddles can also correct hand placement, teaching swimmers how to get more power on the water. This can be done in freestyle, but also in backstroke and breaststroke (where paddles can be particularly effective). Paddles are not often used for butterfly training, but there are times when they can be used.

Here is a word of caution about paddles. They place more stress on the shoulder joints. Now, swimmers *want* to stress the shoulder joint to make it stronger, but every time swimmers stress body tissue, they must give the tissue time to recover or they will become injured. Coaches and swimmers need to take care not to injure shoulders with too much stress. Work has an additive effect, and swimmers often do a lot of extra things out*side* the pool, like stretching and weights. This is when a parent needs to be mindful. A general rule of thumb is that muscle pain will go away with aerobic work while joint pain must have rest. So, if it still hurts after warm-up, you may have a stressed joint that needs rest.

Pull-buoys

Usually a pull-buoy is used in conjunction with paddles. A pull-buoy is made from plastic or Styrofoam. This flotation device is worn between a swimmer's legs, above the knees, just under the crotch. Pull-buoys float hips and legs and allow swimmers to concentrate on their arm pulls. There are various sizes, and I would recommend that a swimmer get the smallest one that reasonably fits. Swimmers, especially boys, have a tendency to become what is known as PBD or

Pull-Buoy Dependent. Basically, PBD is when swimmers have taught themselves that they can't swim in workout without the aide of a pull-buoy. There are negative mental effects of PDB. You guessed it; it can lower true expectations, making them slower. I have seen this happen many times. Also, too much pull-buoy work can interfere with the integration of the proper kick.

When swimmers wear a pull-buoy, coaches may have them wear a *strap* around their ankles. Straps and pull-buoys should go together. When swimmers use the two together, a coach can detect whether their pull patterns are causing any sideways motions that are compensated for by their kicks. Straps *can* also be used *without* a pull buoy to work on body position—high hips, press the chest down. This is difficult, but worth the effort for older swimmers. Very young swimmers have a hard enough time keeping their hips high without tying their feet together.

Swimming Equipment Wrap-up

So now you know what goes in that mesh bag. By the way, you *do* want to get a bag to keep all the equipment in and a mesh one is best because it breathes and allows wet items to dry.

Here are a few more things for the bag. Every swimmer should have a water (or sports drink) bottle at every practice. In addition to a water bottle, a towel, of course, is a must and sometimes a snack for right after practice makes a nice treat. One with a lot of carbohydrates (remembering the chapter on nutrition) is the best choice.

EIGHT

PREPARING FOR A SWIM MEET

I have covered what swimmers do physically and mentally to prepare for a meet, as well as nutritional considerations of meet preparation. There is much more to a swim meet, however, when you consider it entails a family hanging out at a pool for a day. In this chapter
I will cover these additional swim meet preparations, including what
to do and bring, understanding heat seeding, shaving down and tapering.

The first thing to *do* is arrive at the meet at least 15 minutes prior
to the start of warm-up (the coach should let you know when this is).
This way you can get your location staked out, and your swimmers in
their suits and ready. Warm-up is very important for several reasons.
Warm-up gets swimmers mentally and physically ready to race well
in the meet. It helps swimmers get used to the pool atmosphere, flag
position, wall visibility and texture (some are slippery) and the starting blocks. Perhaps most importantly, however, it allows swimmers
the chance to mentally go over their races while in the meet environment. Cutting warm-up short because you arrive at the pool late is a
bad thing.

While your swimmer is in the pool warming-up, you can "set up
shop." This should include chairs for all, maybe a blanket, looking at

or buying a heat sheet or meet program and writing down event numbers, laying out a towel and the clothes your swimmer might put on between events to stay warm, and finally, setting out snacks and a drink bottle. When warm-up is over, you can write event numbers on your swimmer's hand or arm. This is a relatively new innovation, which seems to work well. Some parents use a ballpoint pen while others use a permanent marker. The ballpoint pen may require more pressure than the permanent marker, but the ink is more easily erased. There is no reason for swimmers to wear a list of their events for the next school week. Besides, if it is more than a one-day meet, it will help to be able to erase or at least fade the ink marks from the previous day. Here is an example of how to write their events.

Event	Name	Heat	Lane
11	Med R	2	3
19	100 free	7	1
29	50 back	8	4
43	100 fly	4	6
51	Free R	2	5

After your swimmer is marked, it is helpful to arrange all the things needed to swim the meet. The items you've already laid out are not required to actually swim. The items actually required to swim are generally *on* your swimmer during warm-up. If your swimmer has a cap, either get it on or get it in a place where it can be put on before the first race. Have a place for the goggles to go so that when your swimmer is finished swimming, goggles can be put in this place (like tucked under the leg hole of the swimming suit). This saves a panicked search for goggles right before a race. Once children learn organization at a swim meet, it will help them throughout their swimming careers and perhaps spill over into other things (but don't count on a cleaner room).

Most coaches like to talk with swimmers both before and after each of their swims. Parents can help or hurt this process. When parents ask their swimmer, "What are you going to concentrate on during this race?" or "What did the coach tell you to think about?" they are likely to reinforce what the coach tells their swimmer. When parents tell their swimmer to concentrate on something other than what the coach told their swimmer, they're courting overload. Most swimmers can take one thought into the water and still swim fast. Having too many things to concentrate upon can slow them down. For most parents it is best to not say anything technical to their children about swimming *during* a meet (sometimes even *after*wards). If your swimmer seems to want encouragement, go for it. Otherwise, give your swimmer a chance to compete without your assistance.

Once your child is finished swimming an event, you need to be mindful of what you say. Don't get *too* overjoyed if the swim goes well and don't be *too* disappointed if it goes poorly. Just be supportive at all times. If you only say something when your child does well and nothing when your child does poorly, then silence indicates to your swimmer that you think the performance was poor. Generally, swimmers will do at least *something* well in each race. If you know what your child was working on and that was done well, who cares about the time? You can comment on what your child was trying to do. This keeps you away from the time game and may help your *child* focus on things other than time too. Whatever parents do, they should never show anger at a child's swimming performance. Parents may be angry if they think a child is not trying, but they should never let their swimmer see that anger. When parents show anger at towards their swimmer's performance, their swimmer's career will be very short. Remember that this is your child's swimming, not yours.

During a meet, swimmers will spend much more time hanging out than actually swimming. It is important that they have something fun and productive to do. I personally do not favor Gameboys® and other electronic distractions. Leave these items at home and don't let your swimmer watch or play with anyone else's. These games are addictive and many young swimmers (especially boys) will miss their heats or be distracted from their events because their minds are on the electronic games. They haven't trained for hours in the pool to perfect their Gameboy® skills during a meet. These games can also lead to fights or bad feelings. Swimmers who prefer to be isolated can read books (which help them in school and expand their imaginations and vocabularies).

Games like cards, Yatzee® or other interactive games can keep the group occupied and provide good interaction between several swimmers. The amount of concentration for these games is not as intense as it is for electronic games and children only have so much concentration. Better that concentration be spent on their races. Interactive games also help them bond as a team, which is good for any number of reasons. If several swimmers bring their favorite games, then they'll always have something to do and time will fly between events. An added benefit to games is that swimmers will look forward to swimming meets as much for the interaction with peers as for the swimming. Either way, if they look forward to a meet, that's a good thing.

What to bring to a meet depends partly on whether it's indoors or outdoors. If the meet is outdoors, your swimmer needs to be kept in the shade to avoid sunburn, overheating or loss of energy due to the sun. Sometimes pools are built beside parks, which may provide trees for shelter. If you know this to be the case, fine. If not, then it's best to provide your *own* shade with a canopy. A canopy can also protect the family from rain. In addition to shade, sunscreen is a must at outdoor swimming meets. Use the strong stuff, because even though the bottle may say, "Doesn't wash off," this means with a dip in the pool, not someone swimming at full speed for several laps. You never know how much really will wash off.

During the meet, if there is an additional warm-up and warm-down pool, then it is good for swimmers to swim a few laps easy after each race. A warm-down can help remove lactic acid that builds up inside their muscles during a race. It can also be a good idea for swimmers to warm *up* before a race with a few laps, especially if they haven't swum for 45 minutes or longer. Again, this is just a "loosen and warm-up the muscles" process where swimmers can also do a few turns to mentally get ready for their races.

Some parents will want to take a logbook and write down their swimmer's times. Unless your child demands this, it isn't necessary. I probably won't stop anyone from checking out the results board, but parents shouldn't get too caught up in times. This will be a bad thing for your swimmer in the long run. No matter how hard anyone concentrates on time, it passes at the same rate. We can't swim faster by slowing time down. The things that make a swimmer faster have been covered in earlier chapters. If a parent pays attention to anything, it should be to technique. Paying attention to swimming times places emphasis on the wrong thing. Place your emphasis on what gets results—the process of good swimming.

A Checklist of Items to Bring to a Swim Meet

Racing swimsuit—should be *worn* to the meet if the meet is within an hour of home.
Practice suit – just in case.
Goggles, 2 pairs (tightened for racing)
Swim caps (2) if desired
Towels (2)
Kickboard (only if used during warm-up)
Sweat suit (in case of cool conditions)
Sunscreen (if outdoors)
Hat (if outdoors)
Snacks
Drinks
Flip-flops (easy on-off between swims)
Chairs (one for each member of the family)
Books (for adults too, or maybe the newspaper)
Games
Pens for marking
Money

Heat Seeding

How do swimmers get placed in lanes and heats? Swimmers are placed in their heats and lanes by entry time. There are three ways of doing this and it depends on the meet which method is used. A dual meet with another team is the easiest. One team will get the odd lanes of the pool, the other the even lanes. The visiting coach gets to choose between odd and even. The coaches for each team will then place their swimmers in any of their team's lanes. Normally, they place their fastest swimmers in the middle lanes to be next to the other team's fastest, but there are times when they'll place their fastest swimmer in one of the outside lanes to be out-of-sight of the other team's fastest swimmer.

In general, there are two other types of meet formats—the invitational with no finals and the invitational with finals. These meets are normally held in six or eight-lane pools. For the invitational with no finals, the fastest swimmer is seeded in the middle lane (lane #3 in a six-lane pool and lane #4 in an eight-lane pool). The rest of the swimmers are then seeded inside to outside around the heat's fastest swimmer. In an eight-lane pool, it might look like this:

Lane #8	8th fastest	(1:04.50)
Lane #7	6th fastest	(1:04.25)
Lane #6	4th fastest	(1:03.10)
Lane #5	2nd fastest	(1:02.00)
Lane #4	Fastest swimmer	(1:01.00)
Lane #3	3rd fastest	(1:02.50)
Lane #2	5th fastest	(1:03.70)
Lane #1	7th fastest	(1:04.26)

Championship meets *with* finals have a different seeding process for the preliminaries. The last three heats of the preliminaries are specially seeded. All preliminary heats other than the final three are seeded as described in the previous section. The final three preliminary heats are seeded with the fastest swimmer in lane four of the *last*

heat (eight lane pool), the second fastest swimmer in lane four of the
second to last heat and the third fastest in lane four of the *third* to last
heat. Mapping out the top 24 swimmers in an eight-lane pool would
look like this:

3rd to last heat

Lane #8 24th fastest
Lane #7 18th fastest
Lane #6 12th fastest
Lane #5 6th fastest
Lane #4 3rd fastest
Lane #3 9th fastest
Lane #2 15th fastest
Lane #1 21st fastest

2nd to last heat

Lane #8 23rd fastest
Lane #7 17th fastest
Lane #6 11th fastest
Lane #5 5th fastest
Lane #4 2nd fastest
Lane #3 8th fastest
Lane #2 14th fastest
Lane #1 20th fastest

Last heat

Lane #8 22nd fastest
Lane #7 16th fastest
Lane #6 10th fastest
Lane #5 4th fastest
Lane #4 Fastest swimmer
Lane #3 7th fastest
Lane #2 13th fastest
Lane #1 19th fastest

The timed results from the preliminary heats will then create the seeding for the final heats. Again, using an eight-lane pool, the eight fastest swimmers are seeded in the championship heat of the finals with the fastest qualifier in lane four, second fastest in lane five, third fastest in lane three and so on. There is usually a consolation final where swimmers whose preliminary times placed them 9th-16th can swim. In this case, the 9th place swimmer is the fastest in the heat and therefore will be seeded in lane four. The others are placed in lanes that follow the previously described pattern around the fastest swimmer. Sometimes there is a bonus final where the 17th-24th fastest can swim.

It often happens that the winner of (and maybe other swimmers) in a consolation final, record a time faster than some of the swimmers in the championship final. No matter how fast the winner of the consolation final swims, that swimmer can only be 9th place. Even if a swimmer is disqualified in the championship final, the winner of the consolation final can only be 9th place. No matter how slow the 8th place finisher in the championship final swims, that swimmer can only be 8th place. If there is a bonus final, it works the same way where no swimmer can move up higher than 17th place.

The Shave Down

Shaving down entails the removal of most of a swimmer's body hair. Swimmers may shave their arms, armpits, chests, backs, legs and heads for a swim meet. Shaving removes body hair that causes drag. It also exposes nerve endings, making skin more sensitive. Physically, less drag means faster swimming. Psychologically, the tactile sensation of no body hair makes swimmers feel faster in the water. Because of this, shaving can dramatically change swimmers' true expectations and they'll swim faster in fact.

So how old should a swimmer be to start shaving down? Even though 12 and under children have body hair, I don't generally recommend that they shave down. Will shaving help them swim faster?

Possibly. But save the shaving until later in your child's swimming career when the stakes are higher. Don't get into the habit early of having the one big meet each year where it is important to swim fast and the rest of the meets are unimportant. Shaving can sometimes signify this to a swimmer. Shaving down is ultimately up to the coach and parent. It kind of falls into the same category as the Fastskin suit. The Fastskin suit makes swimmers feel like they are shaved. Swimmers who aren't old enough for a Fastskin suit are not ready to shave either.

But for swimmers who *are* going to shave, how is it done? Probably the best way to shave is to initially use hair clippers to get off any *long* hair. After that, a bladed razor is used. Some swimmers use shaving cream, some shave in the tub or shower, some do it dry. Shaving dry may cause a rash, but tends to cause greater sensation once in the water. Sometimes swimmers use sandpaper (100 grit) on the palms of their hands to increase or change their feel of the water. Rubbing the palms across the rough surface of the starting block before a race has the same effect.

The Taper

A taper is a reduction in workload, in this case a reduction of swimming distance per practice. Swimming programs will "taper" their swimmers when they want them to be rested and sharp for a meet. Tapers usually correlate with faster swimming times for several reasons, but one of the biggest is that swimmers feel more energetic and that feeling leads to greater confidence and expectations of what they can do in the water.

Young swimmers age 10 and under are usually not affected by a taper since they don't swim that far (over-train) in practice, making it difficult to reduce their workloads. During taper time, these younger swimmers will do more starts and turns than usual to sharpen the technical aspects of their races. Older swimmers will not only reduce distances per practice—taper—but also spend more time working at race pace.

What parents need to know about tapers is that swimmers will feel more energetic. They won't burn all their calories in workouts, so may look to use that energy in other pursuits. They may want to play basketball, go for runs, or pick on their siblings more than usual. None of these activities is good for their taper.

Here is an opportunity for a parent to help the swimmer. The coach can't be with a swimmer 24-hours a day, but a parent can help during non-practice hours. A taper is a good time to do low stress activities like catch up on movies. I recommend feel-good sport's movies because they are often highly motivating and have a way of getting into swimmers' psyches and positively changing true expectations.

The most important thing for swimmers to do during a taper period is sleep. Swimmers should try to get extra sleep every night prior to the taper meet. This may be difficult, because they probably won't feel as tired and extra sleep means going to bed earlier. But get your swimmers to bed early. An hour more sleep each night usually means feeling better. Feeling better means faster swimming both in the practices before a big meet and during the big meet itself.

Swim Meet Prep Wrap-up

Different levels of meets require different preparation. Swim meets will often be all day events involving most of the family. So, it is best to make everyone comfortable and have something for everyone to do. Write your own checklist of what to bring and set up a routine to keep things consistent for your swimmer no matter where the meet is located. If swimmers are tapering, make sure they get lots of rest. If they plan to shave, get them some new razors. Then sit back and be ready for some fast swims and some big smiles.

NINE

SWIMMING BURNOUT

"No matter how hard I train, I don't get any better." "Do I have to go to practice?" "I get physically sick when I show up at workout." "I really don't like to race anymore." "I hate swimming!" If you hear these comments from your swimmer, you may be dealing with *burn-out*.

Some parents have turned to this chapter *first* because their swimmer is experiencing burnout right now and they are looking for solutions. Others are reading this chapter to help prevent their child from burning out sometime in the near future. Yet others haven't even considered the possibility of burnout for their young swimmers. This chapter is for all of you.

Burnout can be defined as a psychological, emotional and at times physical withdrawal or desire to withdraw from an activity, in this case swimming. It is not difficult to get inside a swimming circle and find burned-out swimmers. In fact, swimmers probably have a higher ratio of burnout than any other athletic group. Many college level swimmers are burned-out, but must continue swimming because swimming pays for their educations. This is a sad situation. Very few of these swimmers will continue to swim after they graduate. Most begin counting down the days to their last swim practice during their senior year. This is burnout, psychological, emotional and physical exhaustion. And it happens *before* college too.

Why Swimmers Get Burned-out

Swimming is not like many team sports. Practices are not games and drills, they're workouts. Swim workouts can be physically and mentally grueling and create lots of stress. Over-stress is one of the major causes of burnout. Two other causes of burnout that will be discussed are what I call the "Swimming Paradigm" and stagnation.

Over-stress can come from several sources. When swimmers are in the water swimming, they are alone. A lot of swimmers like workout because they get to see friends, but when their faces are underwater there's not much communication going on. There is camaraderie in working out together, but essentially swimmers are there to endure hardship and physical stress.

In swimming, winning and losing is based solely on the swimmer. In team sports, there are several teammates with whom to share that joy or burden. Individual sports can therefore place greater amounts of emotional stress on individuals by putting responsibility for their performances solely on them.

Swimming is exhausting. If workouts are too hard, that in itself can cause burnout. And swimming is not the only activity in which swimmers engage. School, family, church, friends, other sports and interests—these in addition to swimming are often too much for anyone. Being over-scheduled can cause over-stress and burnout.

I believe another cause of burnout is the "Swimming Paradigm." The Swimming Paradigm asserts that experienced swimmers should train all year, once or twice a day, and at the end of the season, shave, taper and reduce their times in a two-minute race by half a second—and be happy about the improvement. This paradigm seems to be completely entrenched in swimming at the high levels. Coaches will tell their swimmers that at the beginning of the season they are going to tear them down and that they won't be swimming well, but that it will be okay, because at the end of the season, they'll build them back up and they'll swim personal records (PR's), dropping five tenths of a second or so from their best times. Now that's if everything goes according to the plan. What happens when it doesn't? The swimmer has a year without improving. Is that depressing? That's depressing! Moreover, what does this paradigm do to a swimmer's true expectations? If the coach says a swimmer is not going to swim fast in a meet because that swimmer's muscles will be torn down at a specific point in the season, the swimmer's true expectations are likely to fulfill that prophecy. Gone are the days where swimmers thought they could swim a PR every time they got on the blocks. No swimmer ever complained about burnout after swimming a best time.

Obviously the Swimming Paradigm, which many of you parents have experienced and the others of you *will*, is very harmful to good swimming and the mental wellbeing of swimmers. Unfortunately, there is little you, as a parent, can do about it. You can talk to your swimmer—there are always rogue swimmers out there who dare to be different and swim fast even when others don't expect them to. You can talk to your coach and try to get them to think outside their "swimming box". It's hard to think "out of the box." If you are lucky enough to have a coach who does this, don't ever change teams—you have a winner. Whatever your situation, the current swimming paradigm is something our swimming community must change.

Probably the major cause of older swimmer burnout is stagnation. Swimming stagnation occurs when little or no improvement is made in swimming times over a sustained period. When swimmers are young they have so many things they can improve and just changing *one* allows them to swim faster almost every time they get in the water. They do a best time in at least one event at every meet. This is fun for swimmers and after a while they learn to expect this improvement. It can keep coming too, as swimmers grow older, wiser, taller and stronger. But inevitably, there is a plateau where their times stop improving. That is when stagnation occurs. It can happen anytime from age 10 on.

What to do With Burned-out Swimmers

So, now I have explained some of the reasons swimmers *get* burned-out. What if you have a swimmer who *is* burned-out? Sometimes, perhaps most of the time, the best thing to do is let your swimmer quit. This may be a temporary break or a permanent one. No matter what parents do, they can't *force* a child to want or love to swim. This has to come from within the child. So, if a child is burned-out and wants to quit swimming, you should probably allow them to do so. This may not be the answer you were expecting here, but if you don't let your child quit and you force that child to swim, your parent-child relationship could be jeopardized. The sport of swimming isn't worth that. Every situation is a bit different and as the parent, you will ultimately have to evaluate what is best for your own child's wellbeing.

A less drastic solution, particularly for more experienced swimmers is to give swimmers more say in their training. This may help if the swimmer is burned-out because of stagnation. Once swimmers have been training and competing a few years, they possess a great deal of knowledge about themselves. John Naber, one of the greatest swimmers of the past century, once said that swimmers were their own best coaches, that swimmers know exactly what they need to do to get better, but that they need a coach to enforce it. (I hope I remembered that correctly, John. If not, it still holds true.) Older swimmers may know what they need to do to get better. There are no competitive athletes who don't *want* to get better. No one spends time swimming to get worse. If your swimmer *is* burned-out, then he/she should approach the coach and ask about input. This input might consist of favorite sets or specific drills that the swimmer believes will help them.

Yet another option that works for some swimmers with burnout is to change strokes. This can help to reduce both stress and stagnation. Swimmers pick their worst stroke and train for improvement in that stroke. When they swim a meet, they swim that stroke only. The good part of this is that swimmers will start off with low expectations, which should be easily realized. The stress associated with winning or doing a best time is temporarily gone. It is usually easy to improve in an off event with concentrated practice, and most swimmers get a bit excited about that and feel perhaps a long absent taste of success and accomplishment. This can only be done with coach approval, because the coach is the one who sets up workouts and meets. Ninety-nine percent of age-group coaches will do this. Since swim coaching doesn't pay very well, most coaches are in it for the kids and have the kids' best interests at heart.

I Can See Burnout on the Horizon

Parents who can see burnout on the horizon need to ask themselves and their swimmers why this is the case. The answers will guide their reactions. Help should be sought for swimmers who haven't been improving. The first thing to do is to talk with the coach. The coach may have some answers. Either way, good communication between parent, swimmer and coach is important, because swimmers who think the coach doesn't notice them will be less motivated and more prone to burnout in the first place.

One of the best ways to help a child on the edge of burnout is to employ the aid of a sports psychologist. This can be an expensive option, but there are some out there who can make a world of difference with regular contact. Remember what I said earlier about high-level swimming being 90% mental, so it makes sense to consult a mental expert. By the way, this is not a sign of weakness. Olympians and professional athletes are regulars with sports psychologists. They learn to be mentally stronger, which makes them physically stronger.

Another, perhaps less expensive option if you live by a university that has a graduate program in sports psychology, is to have a graduate student work with your child. Graduate students are usually on the cutting edge of sports psychology, lacking only experience. Your child helps the graduate student get experience and the graduate student helps your child. Obtaining sports psychology help is clearly not an option for everyone, but I would be remiss if I didn't list it because I have seen sports psychologists do great things for athletes.

If finding a sports psychologist is not the right option for you, then think about getting a *book* on sports psychology. There are also instructional audio tapes that are probably available at your local library. Time spent building up the mental strength of your child is time well spent.

Another option to avoid imminent burnout is time off for the swimmer before it happens. Take a season off, perhaps a year, depending on the child's age. Timing depends on the swimmer's goals. If the goal is to swim in college, then a swimmer's junior and senior years of high school are pretty important, because that's when NCAA (university) coaches will be looking at them. NCAA coaches can't *recruit* swimmers until their senior years in high school, so they are looking at the *times* swum during a swimmer's junior year. Here is a secret. NCAA coaches look for swimmers who improve between their junior and senior years. Swimmers that improve tend to have bright college swimming careers; swimmers who don't are often facing burnout. Some swimmers may take a season off during their freshman years of high school or perhaps only swim for three months that year during the high school season. If they come back refreshed and loving swimming, it was time well spent away.

Working with burnout depends on the swimmer's goals, not the parents'. Olympic Swimmer Dara Torres was swimming her best times when she was 14 and 15 years old. She swam in the 1984 Olympics. She then made the 1988 Olympic team and competed in those Olympics before retiring. After some time off, she came out of retirement to make and compete in the 1992 Olympics. Then she retired again. Seven years later she came out of retirement and trained for one year to make the 2000 Games. In those Games, she was 33 years old and setting U.S. swimming records. This is a great lesson for all swimmers for a number of reasons. First, someone with good technical swimming skills and an excellent competitive mind does not lose them even after a seven-year layoff. Another is that a swimming

111

career doesn't have to be from ages 6-22. In fact, swimming is a life-time sport. It doesn't have to end post high school or college. Master's swimming starts at age 19 and goes for as long as you can get wet. There are masters swimmers today who are between the ages of 50 and 80 who have never stopped swimming and enjoying the benefits it provides. Instead of doing the 6-22 year span, swimming should be a 6-100+ career. And as you can see, it doesn't have to be continuous. Breaks can be both refreshing and motivating.

I Don't Want My Young Swimmer to Burnout

As stated before, one of the key elements of burnout is stress. Stress is an individual thing and what may stress one child will not stress another. Stress can be good or bad. Without stress we would not likely accomplish much, but *too* much stress is associated with many psychological and physical problems, burnout being one of them. Parents need to know how much stress their child is feeling, both in everyday swim practices and at meets. Do they love to go? Do they get very excited? Do they swim for socialization? Do they hate practices because they don't like to work hard? Do they get miserably nervous before meets?

Obviously, if your swimmer is excited to go to practices and meets, you are not currently facing a problem and you may never do so if you keep things in moderation. If your swimmer is seemingly, "going through the motions," it could go either way. A lot of swimmers who are just going through the motions early in their swimming careers become outstanding swimmers. They come on in swimming at ages 13-17 as their bodies and minds begin to develop. On the other hand, they could fall out of swimming just as easily. The ones who hate it now (say we're talking up to about 12 years old) probably won't make it, but I have some suggestions for them too.

Children who love to swim and are doing very well, both in times and technique, need to be protected from stagnation. Check out the records for 8 and under and 9-10 and even 11-12 year olds and see how many names made it to the Olympics? If you don't have the re-cords in front of you, don't bother looking at them, because I can tell you that you won't recognize anyone. It would be interesting to know how many of those record holders completed a four-year college swimming career and how many quit by age 15. Having great success early in swimming can actually be detrimental. I say this having a child who just won the 8 & Under Championships in 4 events. Very few young champions hang on. Most of them fade away, and for the most part the reason is stagnation.

One easy way to prevent such stagnation is to not have your young superstar swimmer swim year round. This is a very hard thing to do for all concerned. Both coaches and parents tend to get it into their heads that they have this eight-year old superstar and if their swimmer keeps improving at this rate, they'll have an Olympic Champion by the age of 14. Forget these thoughts! Your swimmer will not be a 14-year old Olympic Champion. They are much more likely to be a burnout statistic. But let's just say your child *does* be-come an Olympic Champion at age 14. *Is* this a good thing? Probably not. Fourteen-year olds (15 too) rarely have the maturity to handle such success. Probably some 18-year olds have the maturity to handle all that comes with being an Olympic Champion at such a young age, but even many of them do not. Fame and fortune (which may or may not come with swimming) is not usually a good thing for people of any age, and it can change their lives in some very unpleasant ways. Too much success as children often leads to very unhappy adults be-cause it is hard to live up to others' (and their own) expectations. So the point is that young swimmers will be bigger, stronger and smarter as they get *older*. Swimmers don't need to do everything in swim-ming while they are young.

Suppose a young champion swimmer takes some time off, per-haps just participates in the summer season. This time off will give the young swimmer a chance to do other sports or activities. During this time, the swimmer will grow taller and stronger. When this swimmer comes back to swimming bigger, stronger and remotivated, the sport will be new and challenging.

If a young champion (say Terre, a hot shot 9-year old) *is* going to swim year round, the coach needs to safeguard her right from the start. This should be clear between the coach and the parents so that the parents understand why the coach is doing what should be done. Terre could work different strokes every six months. For the first six months, a lot of freestyle, for the next six months concentration on backstroke and so on. When she goes to meets, she swims the last two strokes she concentrated on and no others. This should be done even if it means not getting high point or swimming her best event or swimming as many events as the meet allows. Again, communication in this case is important because it can be difficult for parents and the child to understand why the child is not getting high point or swimming her best event or winning as they have come to expect.

Another thing both parents and coaches can do is limit the number of meets a young champion swims. The idea here is to limit the number of times the swimmer swims specific events. In a swimming career, a freestyler may swim the 100 freestyle over 1000 times. This is not likely to be a positive thing. By limiting races, one limits the chance of stagnation, as the swimmer will grow and mature as time (3 months) passes. Now this is not *always* a good idea, because most young swimmers swim because they love to race and when racing is limited or taken away, they lose motivation to practice. So the coach and parent should keep their eyes on the swimmer and limit the swimmer to only the meets the swimmer needs to stay motivated.

Burnout Wrap-up

Over-stress, the Swimming Paradigm and stagnation are three major causes of burnout in swimming. Some solutions to burnout are quitting, taking time off, more swimmer input, changing strokes, limiting races and professional psychological help. If your swimmer is burnt-out now, you must find a solution now. If not, please be mindful of the potential pitfalls that can cause burnout so your swimmer can continue a lifetime of swimming enjoyment.

T E N

LETTING THE COACHES DO THEIR JOBS

Rule #1, "The coach is always right." Rule #2, "If you don't think the coach is right, refer back to Rule #1." This is an important pair of rules for your swimmer. We all know the coach *isn't* always right—they're human. However, young swimmers need to believe in their coaches. If they do, then the coach can instill great confidence in them. Confidence is more important than technique, sorry to say, because confidence *directly* changes true expectations in a positive way. So, the coach, even if wrong, is right.

I hope you've read to this point of the book before you've taken it to your child's coach and said, "You're doing it wrong, see what it says in this book!" This book is not written to make you the expert in swimming. Having read this book does not mean that you now know more than your child's coach. You don't want to be the "Little league parent" who gets in arguments with your child's coach over every little thing. I hope my comments throughout this book have conveyed how bad this would be for your swimmer, as well as the other members of the team.

That doesn't mean you can't talk to your child's coach about your swimmer in a non-confrontational way. But in the long run, if you don't like the coach's methods, change teams rather than trying to change the coach. Find the best situation for your child. That's your right and responsibility. Different coaches have different styles and one style might fit your child better than another. If so, that's the environment your child needs. Of course, parents often have more than one child in the family who swims and most times these children will have different personalities. There are parents out there who have their children on different teams because one child does well with one coach while the other does well with another coach or team. This is logistically and sometimes financially difficult until kids can drive themselves to workouts, but parents sometimes do it because they see what works best for their children. Hopefully, though, you will find a coach flexible enough to work with many different personalities and with whom your kids can develop great relationships.

Many parents really want to be involved with their child's swimming and swim team. They look to constantly talk to the coach and get feedback about their swimmer. They want to give the coach suggestions about what races they think their child should swim. Some of this is good, but some goes overboard. If a coach has 60 swimmers on a team and there are 30 sets of parents for those swimmers and the coach talks to every one of them at every workout for say five minutes each, then that's two and a half hours of talk. If this is going on during practice, then the kids aren't getting coached. Parents often find that they get one or two lines of conversation with a coach, which is more, "How are you today?" than anything about the kids. If parents want more, they should set up a time to talk with the coach *outside* practice. Buy the coach a meal at a swim meet between sessions and talk with them then. Also, coaches have families and usually need family time; so calling at night might not be a good idea. A coach will let you know when is best for communication. An e-mail to the coach might be good because the coach can answer when time permits.

The best way to help your swimmer's coach and team is to volunteer. Coaches have a tremendous amount of administrative work. Administrative work comes with any coaching job, but I have yet to hear a coach say, "I got into coaching because I love the admin work." If you are willing to take on some of this work, you'll probably have more communication with the coach and your child and all the kids will get more of the coach's time.

Some parents have a great deal of swimming experience and can help the coach technically. Such a parent might suggest they guest coach a lane on occasion (usually not with their child in it). Then the coach would have more time with the other swimmers, including that parent's child. Parents wishing to do this need to approach it carefully and they must work underneath the coach and not around or above them. A great way a coach can use swim knowledgeable parents is to have them watch a lane for technique. Parents can sit at either end of the pool and watch turns to make sure all the swimmers streamline and take a stroke before their first breath. This can really help a team's technique improve quickly, though care must be taken not to disrupt the practice.

It is often the case, with any team or situation, that a parent or outsider can look at the team and say, "It would be better if . . ." If you have said this about your child's swim team, here is a suggestion. Ask yourself what you could do to help correct the problem. If you can do something about it, then see if the coach/team would like that. If you can't or don't have time to do anything about it, then it's better that you don't complain.

If you don't like the way a coach is performing some aspect of the job, I caution you to be very careful about expressing this around your swimmer. It is very harmful for swimmers to hear negative comments about their coaches from a parent. Remember, "The coach is always right." Swimmers see both coaches *and* parents as authority figures and as a parent you would not want the coach undermining *your* authority. Moreover, swimmers talk to each other and things that you say may affect other swimmers' attitudes towards the coach which would be unfair to both the other swimmers and to the coach. If you believe that it would be better for your child to swim elsewhere, you should never tell your child that you are switching teams because of a coach (even if that's the reason). You may tell your swimmer that the practice times are better on another team, or that you wanted him/her to be with friends, etc. Even if you move to another team, you and your swimmer will see the former coach at nearly every meet and your swimmer will likely have a great deal of contact with swimmers from their old team. Beyond that, when swimmers think they can change to a different team every time *they* don't like the coach (or something that the coach does), then they feel they have the power to do what they please in workouts and this is very unproductive. I have seen swimmers move to a different team every year, until by the time they enter college, they have had over ten coaches. These are not happy swimmers and are nightmares for their subsequent college coaches. These swimmers' parents have taught them that no coach is good enough for them. Think of all the negative ramifications of this situation that can go far beyond swimming.

Remember that a parent's relationship with the coach is not paramount. A *swimmer's* relationship with the coach *is*. Swimmers can become very attached to their coaches because they feel that their coach's eyes are on them for the entire time they are in the water. I have said that swimming can be a lonely sport, but while swimmers' faces are in the water, they are often thinking of the coach and that the coach is watching them. This creates a tight bond between swimmers and their coaches. The relationship is usually a healthy one and many swimmers will maintain contact with their coaches for the rest of their lives.

Coaches are teachers not only of sports; they are teachers of life. Many of us can remember a teacher or coach who significantly and positively affected our lives. These are very special people. They don't do it for the money or the glory. Swim coaching seldom provides these things. They do it for your child. They do it for the sport of swimming because they know that swimming can teach children so many lessons, lessons that shape them into great adults. Age group coaches for all sports are some of the best people with whom we can ever hope for our children to interact.

Because coaches can stay with an athlete for several years, their impact on a swimmer's life can be immeasurable. They make great sacrifices of their own personal time for your swimmers. Don't forget to thank them. Hopefully your child won't forget either. To this end, *I* would like to thank Paul Arata, Rick Unks, Lois Claus and Henry Weinbecht. They are, each one of them, a part of this book, because the lessons they taught have become a part of me. Their impact on *my* life *has* been immeasurable.

FINAL THOUGHTS

Success in swimming depends on the definition one places on the word success. It is more than just winning races. And far more important than a child's success in swimming is your relationship with your child and your child's with you. Swimming can give you a new way to connect perhaps, or just a new arena in which to communicate and interact. It is okay to enjoy your child's swimming and to enjoy watching your child compete. What I caution parents from doing, however, is living their lives through their young swimmer(s). Don't let their successes be *your* success and don't attach your own self-worth to how *they* perform. What a terrible burden that would be for your child. That is not what swimming is about.

Rather, swimming is one of the best opportunities for children to *grow* in many different ways. And you, as a parent, can improve this experience for them. Be open to opportunities to strengthen your child mentally. Support your child's efforts to increase his or her flexibility. Consciously provide good nutrition for your child. Watch for signs of possible burn-out. And finally, go out of your way to cooperate with and help your child's coach

You can be there to experience the failures and the triumphs, including the first time your swimmer finishes a long race, the first time your swimmer wins a heat or an event or even the time your swimmer false starts. You can be there for the personal best and when your swimmer learns how to shake the hand of the kid in the next lane who won the race. Swimming is an incredible teacher.

Children grow up so fast by adult standards. Your child will only be this age once, so make the most of it. Implement the things you have learned in this book. Watch how your child improves. And, by all means, enjoy the time you have with your child, observing as your child learns and progresses in the sport of swimming.

REFERENCES

Arata, A. (1993). Effect of entry angle on the retention of underwater velocity in a swimming start. Masters Thesis. University of Colorado, Colorado Springs.

Ashley C. (2003). Ask the experts. *Splash*. 11(1): 12.

Bak, K. and Magnusson, S. P. (1997). Shoulder strength and range of motion in symptomatic and pain-free elite swimmers. *American Journal of Sports Medicine*. 25(4):454-9.

Bandura, A. (1977). Self-efficacy: Towards a unifying theory of behavioral change. *Psychological Review*, 84, 191-215.

Bandura, A. (1982). Self-efficacy mechanism in human agency. *American Psychologist*, 377, 122-147.

Burke, L. M. (2000). Nutrition for recovery after competition and training. In: *Clinical Sports Nutrition*, 2nd Ed. Burke L. M. and Deakin, V. Editors. McGraw-Hill Australia, Rosevill, NSW.

Cornwell, A., Nelson, A.G. and Sidaway, B. (2002). Acute effects of stretching on the neuromechanical properties of the triceps surae muscle complex. *European Journal of Applied Physiology*. 86(5):428-34.

Costill, D. L., Maglischo, E. and Richardson, A. (1991). *Handbook of Sports Medicine: Swimming*. London: Blackwell Publishing.

Feltz, D. L. and Landers, D. M. (1983). The effects of mental practice on motor skill learning and performance: A meta-analysis, *Journal of Sports Psychology*, 5, 25-27.

Henry, F. M. (1952). Force-time characteristics of the sprint start. *Research Quarterly*, 23:301-18.

Herbert, R. D. and Gabriel, M. (2002). Effects of stretching before and after exercise on muscle soreness and risk of injury. *British Medical Journal*, 325, 468-70.

McMaster, W. C. and Troup, J. (1993). A survey of interfering shoulder pain in United States competitive swimmers. *American Journal of Sports Medicine*. 21(1):67-70.

Mostardi, R., Gandee, R. and Cambell, T. (1975). Multiple daily training and improvement in aerobic power. *Medicine and Science in Sport*. 7, 82.

Nelson, A. G. and Kokkonen, J. (2001). Acute ballistic muscle stretching inhibits maximal strength performance. *Research Quarterly Exercise and Sport*. 72(4):415-9.

Rosenthal, R. and Jacobson, L. (1968). Pygmalion in the classroom. *Teacher expectations and pupil development*. New York: Holt. Rinehart & Winston.

Rovere, G. D. and Nichols, A. W. (1985). Frequency, associated factors, and treatment of breaststroker's knee in competitive swimmers. *American Journal of Sports Medicine*. 13(2):99-104.

Tabrizi, P., McIntyre , W. M., Quesnel, M. B. and Howard, A. W. (2000). Limited dorsiflexion predisposes to injuries of the ankle in children. *Journal of Bone and Joint Surgery*. 82(8):1103-6.

Watt, E., Burkirk, E. and Plotnicki, B. (1973). A comparison of single verse multiple daily regiments. Some physiological considerations. *Research Quarterly*, 44, 119-123.

Weinberg, R. S. (1981). The relationship between mental preparation strategies and motor performance: A review and critique, *Quest*, 33, 195-213.

Willett, W. C. and Stampfer, M. J. (2003). Rebuilding the food pyramid. *ScientificAmerica.com*, Jan.

Wilmore, J. and Costill, D. (1994). *Physiology of Sport and Exercise.* Champaign IL, Human Kinetics, pg 302.

Whitfield, J. (2002). Cold water thrown on warm ups. *Nature New Science*. Macmillan Magazines Ltd.

ABOUT THE AUTHOR

Born in 1961, Alan W. Arata holds a B.S. in Engineering, an M.S. in Exercise Science and a Ph.D. in Biomechanics. Dr. Arata started his swimming career at the "very old" age of 15, but at age 17 won a Colorado High School State Championship. After his collegiate swimming career, he competed in and later coached Modern Pentathlon (swimming, running, fencing, shooting and equestrian). Dr. Arata has coached at the NCAA Division I level in two different sports, netting four NCAA trophies. He is the author of several research articles and was a winner of the Rocky Mountain Fiction Writers Contest for mainstream. He is married to the former Kimberly Dunlop, a nine-time Modern Pentathlon National Champion. They have two children who are both age-group swimmers. Dr. Arata currently teaches as a Professor of Biology and Physical Education and swims several times a week.

NOTES

NOTES

NOTES

NOTES

1785191

Made in the USA